Freedom

from

Emotional Eating

BARB RAVELING

Truthway Press
First Edition 2008
Second Edition 2014
Third Edition 2017

The names and details of the people in the stories of this book have been changed to protect their privacy.

This book is not intended as a substitute for the advice of professional counselors. If you are struggling with a serious issue, please do so under the guidance of a professional counselor and/or physician.

ISBN 978-0-9802243-4-4

Contents

Preface

Welcome to the third edition of *Freedom from Emotional Eating!* I hope God will use it to help you break free from emotional eating. I decided to put out a new edition of the book because the chocolates on the cover of the second edition were tempting too many people to break their boundaries!

I also made some minor edits, but if you're using the book with a group, it won't matter which edition of the book you use, as very little has changed since the book was first published in 2008. Since I get so many people asking me what the difference is between the three weight loss books I've written, I thought I'd share that below:

- *Freedom from Emotional Eating*: This book deals mostly with letting go of the negative emotions that make us overeat. The comment I get most often with this book is that yes, it helped me with eating, but even more so, it helped me with life.

- *Taste for Truth: A 30 Day Weight Loss Bible Study*: This is the best book for helping you lose weight and follow your weight loss boundaries. It covers the need for boundaries, the different reasons we overeat, body image, and motivation to follow your boundaries.

- *I Deserve a Donut (And Other Lies That Make You Eat)*: This is an ongoing renewing of the mind resource that you can use on a daily basis to help you follow your eating boundaries and talk to God about life. It's also a companion guide to *Taste for Truth*.

If you'd like to lead this Bible study with a group, you can download a free leader's guide at barbraveling.com under the "Other Resources" tab. If you want to lead the study without the leader's guide, just focus on the questions in the book marked with a small circle when you get together with your group.

My prayer is that God will use this book for good in your life. Begin the Bible study with the introduction as it contains vital information for the rest of the study. If you'd like other resources to help with weight loss, including a podcast devoted to the subject, look for more information at barbraveling.com.

Barb Raveling
December 19, 2016

The Anatomy of an Affair

Emma sat at the kitchen table, her head in her hands. Once again her mind drifted back over the events of the past year. What had she been thinking? She shook her head slowly. It was all because of choir, she thought. If only she hadn't joined the choir . . . if only Jeremy hadn't joined the choir.

She remembered the day he came. Tall, curly hair, athletic build. He looked pretty good for an old guy. Of course, she wasn't interested. Just observant. They had kids the same age, so there was the usual talk about school and sports. He was a nice guy, but she was married. She wasn't looking for a relationship.

That changed the day they stayed late to work on a song. It happened to be the same day she and her husband had a big fight, and she was feeling pretty fragile. She tried to lose herself in the music, but it didn't help.

As Jeremy walked her to the parking lot after practice, he asked her if anything was wrong. Something about the tone of his voice made her start to cry, and before long she was sharing her problems with him. He gave her a hug as they said good-bye, and he promised to pray for her.

That was the beginning. The beginning of a friendship. The beginning of a passion. The beginning of a sin.

Emma hadn't planned on having an affair. She was a Christian. She knew adultery was wrong. Yet, like so many other women, she found herself in the midst of an adulterous relationship without having a clear idea of how it ever happened.

"I know," she told a friend later, "You hear it all the time . . . it just happened. But it really did. Before I stopped to think, I was involved in a full-blown affair. I knew it was wrong, but I couldn't see a way out. So I just made the best of it."

Introduction

Has it ever occurred to you that emotional eating is a bit like having an affair? I know. That sounds extreme. But think about it.

Emma loved spending time with Jeremy. He was comforting. He was fun. He was exciting. Yes, he brought a few worries into her life, but when they were together, he was worth it.

Emma hadn't intended to get involved with him, but once she was, she couldn't make herself end the relationship—even though she knew he had the potential to completely mess up her life. It was almost as if she were obsessed with him.

Is this beginning to sound familiar? Read the last couple of paragraphs again. Couldn't we say the same things about our relationship with food? Overeating may be fun in the moment, but it certainly has its downside.

Let's go back to a comment Emma made: It just happened. Here's my question: Do affairs really just happen, or can they be prevented? Here's another question: Would it have been easier for Emma to prevent the affair before or after the evening she shared her problems with Jeremy?

I think we both know the answer to that question. It would have been far easier to end the relationship in its early stages, before her emotions got involved. The problem was that the relationship didn't seem dangerous in the beginning. Emma felt like she was engaging in an innocent, fun friendship. She didn't foresee the heartache that this relationship would bring to her life.

In order for her to have prevented the affair with Jeremy, she would have had to set boundaries in her relationships with *all* men. This would have kept her from being seriously tempted to commit adultery with one man. Once she became close to Jeremy emotionally, it was very difficult to put the brakes on the progressing relationship.

Boundaries

Let's talk about boundaries for a moment. What exactly is a boundary? A boundary is any restriction we put in place to enhance our lives and keep us safe. Think of a fence at a school playground. The fence is built to protect the children— to keep the kids safe. In like manner, we put up boundaries in our own lives to keep us safe.

One of the boundaries my husband and I have is to pay off our credit card each month. This protects us from the stress of living a debt-filled life, but it also keeps us from doing things we might really like to do.

Now, would it really be that big of a deal to charge something small and not pay it off, say a $50 shirt? Of course not. The problem is that a $50 shirt might lead to a $500 recliner or a $5000 trip to Hawaii, and before you know it we could have a huge credit card debt that *would* be a big deal. Living with strict boundaries in this area makes our lives better—it's worth the sacrifice.

In like manner, Emma's life would have been better if she had had strict boundaries in place regarding her relationships with men. What if she had set and followed this rule: *I will never spend significant time alone with any unrelated man.* Or this one: *I will never discuss intimate matters with another man unless my husband is there.* Do you think the affair would have "just happened" if she'd been practicing those boundaries? I don't think so.

It's easy to see how boundaries in other areas of our lives help us, yet we're often deceived when it comes to food. We think eating is fun, and we only impose boundaries when we want to lose weight. We don't realize how dangerous it is to live without boundaries in this area of our lives. Take a look at the chart below.

	No Boundaries	Boundaries
Belief: Eating what-I-want-when-I-want is fun.	*Our normal lives*	*Our lives when we're trying to lose weight*
Belief: Eating what-I-want-when-I-want is dangerous.		*Our goal*

In reality, it's just as dangerous to eat whenever we feel like eating, as it is to flirt whenever we feel like flirting. Both actions lead to emotional attachments. In order to have lasting change, we need to develop lifelong boundaries in the area of eating, and we need to see them as a good thing.

This will be hard to do since we're already emotionally involved with food. We're not trying to *prevent* an affair—we're trying to end an affair that's already in progress.

Think about it. We eat when we're bored. We eat when we're upset. We eat when we're unhappy. We eat because we want to eat. We eat because it's there to eat. We eat because we *need* to eat.

In truth, we have become emotionally dependent on food. Remember Emma? She didn't get into trouble until her emotions got involved. Unfortunately, we're way past trouble.

So what do we do? We need help, and God is the only one who can help us. Let me explain with the following diagram.

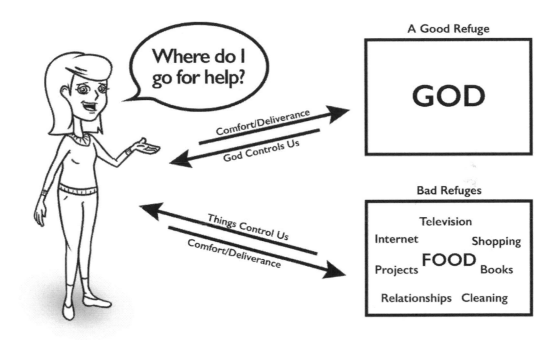

Life isn't always easy. There are things we don't want to do, emotions we don't want to feel, and people we don't want to deal with. Yet we're stuck. We can't always escape our situations. So what do we do? Where do we go for help?

God says, "I'm your refuge—come to me." But it's so much easier to grab a bowl of ice cream, turn on the television, or call a friend. The ice cream will deaden the pain. The television will numb the mind. The friend will listen and feel sorry for us. But God will say, "No wonder you're unhappy. You're not living for me," or "You need to get off the couch and get busy; I have things I want you to do for me today."

The bad refuges don't require anything of us, so they're easy escapes. Going to God for refuge is much more difficult because He *does* ask something of us. He wants us to live for Him, and living for Him isn't always comfortable.

But who's the better refuge? The more we go to God for comfort and help, the more He'll begin to control us. His peace and joy will flood into our lives as we submit to Him (Galatians 5:22-23, Hebrews 12:11).

When we go to other refuges for comfort and help, they also begin to control us. I said that they don't require anything of us, but that's only true in the beginning.

If we go to them too often, they require everything of us for we are no longer in control. They wreak havoc in our lives, yet we can't seem to change our behavior.

These bad refuges are referred to as strongholds in the New Testament. They may actually be good things in our lives, but if we consistently go to them for refuge rather than turning to God, these good things become bad things. Read what 2 Corinthians 10:3-5 has to say about the tearing down of strongholds:

For though we live in the world, we do not wage war as the world does. The weapons we fight with are not the weapons of the world. On the contrary, they have divine power to demolish strongholds. We demolish arguments and every pretension that sets itself up against the knowledge of God, and we take captive every thought to make it obedient to Christ.

Did you notice what I noticed in that passage? Strongholds are not overcome by self-control and discipline, but by taking every thought captive to Jesus Christ. If overeating is a stronghold in your life and not just a weakness, then you'll need to overcome it with the truth. Let's look at another chart.

	Man's viewpoint	**God's viewpoint**
Problem	Weight	Stronghold
Solution	Lose weight	Tear down the stronghold
Method	Diet, exercise	Take every thought captive
Tools (weapons)	Will power, self-control	The Bible, truth

As you can see by this chart, we've been fighting the wrong battle. Not only have we been fighting the wrong battle, we've been using the wrong weapons! No wonder we've failed so many times in our efforts to lose weight and keep it off. If food is a stronghold, we need to use the *truth* to fight against it. Listen to what Jesus said in John 8:32: *Then you will know the truth, and the truth will set you free.*

My friend, God can set you free from emotional eating. As you saturate your mind with truth, God will use the truth to change your desires and actions. We'll explore this idea more in the first week of our study. For now, though, I want to tell you the rest of Emma's story.

The Rest of the Story

Emma was in the grocery store when the news broke. Someone had seen them together, and the secret was out. Her heart sank, and she rushed home to intercept her family before they heard the story from someone else.

There was no question in her mind of what she had to do, and it wouldn't be easy. She tried to stuff down the panic as she drove up to the house. Her husband was working in the garage and the kids were still asleep when she got there. They hadn't heard yet.

She would never forget the look of pain on her husband's face when she told him the truth. The next few hours were heartbreaking. Filled with anguish, disbelief, accusations, and remorse. She didn't regret her relationship with Jeremy, at least not yet, but she certainly regretted what it had done to her family.

Her husband and kids eventually forgave her. They were angry. They were devastated. They were hurt. But they forgave her. Thank God.

She broke off the affair, but it wasn't easy. Some days she missed Jeremy so much it was all she could do to keep from calling him. Somehow she had to find the strength to stay away from him. It helped that people knew about it. They would be holding her accountable.

Emma avoided the places where she might see Jeremy and tried to keep herself busy. She memorized Scripture to help with temptation and worked hard to keep her mind pure. Her intimacy with God grew as she began to rely on Him for her emotional needs.

Eventually she began to see Jeremy with eyes of truth. She thought he had loved her. She came to realize that he had never loved her; he had only desired her. True love wouldn't have been willing to break up a family. And true love wouldn't have encouraged her to sin.

As she began to see Jeremy through eyes of truth, her feelings for him changed. It was no longer hard to stay away from him. She wanted to stay away from him. In fact, she wondered what she had ever seen in him in the first place.

Just as my friend Emma took steps to end her affair with Jeremy, we can take steps to end our affair with food. In fact, why don't we use Emma's methods as our guidelines in this battle?

Steps to Ending an Affair with Food

1. Set Boundaries.

The first thing Emma did was to set boundaries: no more Jeremy. While we can't say "no more food," we *can* say "no more eating what-I-want-when-I-want." We do this by setting lifelong boundaries in the area of food. Lifelong boundaries are boundaries you have in place all the time—not just for a short time to lose weight.

Your lifelong boundaries should limit *how much* and *how often* you eat. There are several ways you can do this, but we'll just focus on two in this book. First, you can limit how much and how often you eat by hunger.

With this set of boundaries, you wait until you're physically hungry (as opposed to emotionally hungry) to eat and you stop eating as soon as you feel physically satisfied (as opposed to emotionally satisfied). *How often* is determined by hunger and *how much* is determined by that feeling of physical satisfaction.

Another way to limit how often you eat is to have a set number of meals and snacks each day. This is what I do. My current boundary is three meals a day. I limit *how much* I eat by putting a healthy amount on my plate and not having seconds unless I plan for them ahead of time, which I usually don't. I know I'm eating the right amount if I'm hungry for the next meal.

In deciding what boundaries to choose, ask yourself this question: *What boundaries would I be willing to live with for the rest of my life?* Experiment with what works best, but keep in mind that there is no perfect set of boundaries that will be easy to follow. If you're an emotional eater, you'll have a hard time following your boundaries no matter how great they are.

Don't worry about that, though, because the more you develop the habit of going to God rather than food for help with life, the easier it will be to follow your boundaries. One day you'll actually *want* to follow them!

If you'd like to set boundaries, record your plan in the space below.

_____

_____

2. Think of your boundaries as absolute boundaries.

Let me ask you a question. What if Emma had said, "Okay, I won't get together with Jeremy again unless I'm really upset." Or "unless I happen to run into him." Or "unless I get a wonderful opportunity to go on an exotic vacation with him."

Do you think she would have been able to break off the affair if she had been that lax with her boundaries? I don't think so. In order to end the affair, she had to have absolute boundaries: no more Jeremy period.

We need to say the same thing if we want to end our affair with food: no more breaking of the boundaries period. That means no licking the spoon while preparing dinner. No eating the crumbs in the brownie pan while walking through the kitchen. And no eating samples at the grocery store unless we plan for them ahead of time.

Yes, I know. It's drastic. But think of Jeremy and Emma. Do "now and then" boundaries really work? Or do they have to be absolute in order to work? What do you think?

_____

3. Learn to rely on God for your emotional needs.

If Emma had gone to God for help with her marriage rather than Jeremy, she probably wouldn't have been tempted to have an affair. It's the same for us with food. If we develop the habit of running to God for help with life rather than food, it will be easier to follow our boundaries.

4. See emotional eating for what it really is.

When Emma saw her relationship with Jeremy through eyes of truth, he wasn't so attractive anymore. She lost her desire to be with him. In like manner, when we see our relationship with food through eyes of truth, we'll lose our desire to eat for emotional reasons. This is accomplished by bringing our thoughts captive to the truth on a regular basis. We'll work on that in the first week of this study.

5. Limit contact with your favorite food, if necessary.

Emma cut off all contact with Jeremy. We can't do that with food or we'd starve to death. But we can cut off contact with the foods that send us over the edge into binge mode.

If you find yourself breaking your boundaries again and again with your favorite foods, consider limiting them or giving them up altogether until you've gotten a little more truth into your system. This is what I did when I was breaking free from the control of food.

My problem foods were sweets and bread with butter. I was okay with the bread as long as I didn't put butter on it. At first I cut sweets and butter out altogether. Then I allowed fruit-based sweets back into my life, only because they didn't tempt me that much.

After a couple of months, I started eating all sweets again, but only on social occasions and holidays. It took me two years to come to the point where I could consistently eat sweets at home as a part of regular life without going overboard with them.

The trick is to do whatever you think has the best chance of keeping you from compulsive eating. If you think it would be easier to cut problem foods out of your life altogether for a season, then do it. If you think that would make you rebel and binge, then keep them as a part of your life.

If you're unsure, ask yourself, "Will this be more likely to *make* me binge or *keep* me from binging?" If you decide to eliminate problem foods, the first week or two will be the hardest. After the initial struggle, the craving seems to go away.

6. Exercise.

If Emma and her husband had spent more time on their relationship, she would have been less tempted to have an affair. Think of exercise as a way you can work on your relationship with your body. Exercise will make you want to be faithful to your body in the way that you eat.

The key is to develop the habit of exercise. You can do this by making a goal to do some form of exercise every day, even if it's just a walk around the block or twenty minutes of yard work. This will get your mind used to the idea that it's important to exercise every day. Once your mind gets used to the idea, you can step up your exercise sessions to make them more active.

How about you? Do you already have an exercise plan? If not, what could you do to add some exercise to your life?

---

7. Memorize Scripture.

Just as exercise gets our bodies in shape, Scripture gets our minds in shape. Memorizing Bible verses will help you break free from the control of food. When you feel like breaking your boundaries, pray through the Bible verses on page 53 of this Bible study as they will help you actually want to follow your boundaries! *I Deserve a Donut* is another helpful resource with lots of Bible verses in it.

8. Avoid boredom.

Emma had to keep herself busy to avoid dwelling on thoughts of Jeremy. Likewise, we need to stay busy so we don't have time to dwell on thoughts of food. If you struggle with boredom eating, skip ahead to page 103 of this study for more ideas on how to handle boredom.

9. Get an accountability partner.

Emma could have ended the affair sooner if she'd had the courage to tell someone about it. There is power in accountability. This could be a Bible study group, a friend, or even a weight loss group.

Can you think of anyone you could ask to be an accountability partner?

---

10. Don't give up.

We've all been there before. We're following our boundaries perfectly. We're starting to fit into our "skinny" clothes. And we're even beginning to feel a little confident. *This set of boundaries is the answer,* we think, as we slip on a pair of jeans we haven't worn in months. *Life is good.*

Then something out of the ordinary happens. Someone has a birthday. A friend brings over a plate of brownies. Or we have one of those days when everything seems to go wrong.

I'll just break it this once, we think. *I've been doing so well. One little cheat won't hurt.* So we break it. And it feels . . . wonderful. So wonderful we decide to break it again. Soon we're *not* doing so well.

Discouragement sets in and that old record begins to play in our minds: *This is just like all the other times. I'll never be able to stick to this. I might as well give up.*

Have you been there? If so, then you know how discouraging it is. I wish I could say, "This time it will be different. This time it will go smooth as silk and you'll wonder why you ever thought it was so hard to lose weight and keep it off."

Unfortunately, I can't say that. It will be hard this time around too. But, here's the difference—and it's a big difference: This time you'll be using spiritual weapons to break free from the stronghold of emotional eating. And those weapons are powerful. God will use the truth to set you free.

Are you ready to begin? Why don't you take a minute to ask God to bless your efforts as you go through this study? Then go ahead and start on the first lesson. I'm excited to see what God will do in your life as you go to Him for help!

Truth

I never knew the value of truth until God began to change my life with it. Yet the teaching of truth permeates Scripture. We're urged to believe the truth, live the truth, and speak the truth.

I guess that begs the question: What is truth? The Bible gives us an answer: God is truth. The Father, Son, and Holy Spirit are all defined by truth (Isaiah 65:16, John 14:6, John 16:13).

God's Word is also defined by truth (John 17:17). As we abide in His Word, He counsels us with truth (Psalm 119:24), He transforms us with truth (Romans 12:2), and He sets us free with truth (John 8:32). Is it any wonder that we begin our study of emotional eating with a study of the truth?

DAY 1

In order to fully understand how the truth can set us free, we must first recognize how a lie can enslave us. Our study of truth then will actually begin with a study of lies. We'll look first at where lies come from, then how they affect us, and finally how we can stop believing them.

Think back to the first time lying appeared in the Bible. Who was lying to whom? (Genesis 3:13)

_____

The world had been created. A wonderful world where Adam and Eve could enjoy fellowship with God in an idyllic setting. Unfortunately, Satan started working on Eve right away to take her out of this perfect world and cause a rift in her relationship with God.

Think of this for a moment. Can you imagine what a daunting task Satan had before him? God had *blessed* Adam and Eve. They had a beautiful place to live and an intimate relationship with God. How could Satan ever get them to give up perfection? Obviously, he needed to come up with a plan of action. What did he decide to do and how did it work? (Genesis 3:1-6)

_____

Did you notice how sneaky Satan was? He didn't come up with an open plan of attack. He knew Adam and Eve would never have gone for it. Instead, he used deceit. His questions made it easier for Eve to rationalize to herself, "Well, maybe that's not *really* what God meant." He also helped Eve to focus on the advantages of disobeying God. Right away, at the beginning of the world, we see how well Satan uses his weapon of deceit to lead us astray.

How is Satan described in the following verses?

John 8:44 _____

Revelation 12:9-10 _____

• If you're anything like me, you've not only been deceived in the area of food, but you've also experienced quite a bit of self-condemnation because of it. In Revelations 12:10, Satan is called the accuser of the saints. Why do you think Satan accuses us?

_____

• How does it affect your weight loss efforts when you beat yourself up after breaking your boundaries?

_____

When we beat ourselves up after breaking our boundaries, our eyes are no longer on God and His life-giving power to transform us. Instead, they're on us and our incredible inability to ever break free from the control of food.

Thankfully, God hasn't left us alone to face Satan's lies and accusations. Instead, He's given us weapons we can use to fight back. Not surprisingly, one of those weapons is the truth.

Read Ephesians 6:10-20 and then look more closely at verse 14. What does Paul tell us to do in that verse?

_____

In the days of Jesus, men wore long robes. These robes got in the way when the men engaged in physical activities, such as fighting. To prepare for battle, a man would reach down and gather up the bottom of his robe, pull it up between his legs, and tie it at his waist with a belt. This was called girding the loins, and it was something that had to be done before going into battle.

Can you imagine a soldier in the middle of a battle saying, "Just a minute, guys! I need to get my robe out of the way!" That's crazy. He'd be dead before he got his belt tied. To be effective, it had to be done *before* going into battle.

Just as soldiers prepared for battle by getting their robes out of the way with a belt, we prepare for *spiritual* battle by getting the lies out of the way with the truth. If we don't put on the truth *before* we go into battle, then we won't be prepared to withstand temptation when it comes. It's essential that we take the time to fill our minds with the truth on a regular basis so that we're ready when Satan attacks.

Read Ephesians 6:10-20 again. What else are you to put on when you prepare for battle?

_____

What is the only offensive weapon mentioned in these verses? _____

In John 17:17 how is the Word of God described?_____

Are you beginning to see how powerful the truth is? Paul talks about using it as both a defensive weapon *and* an offensive weapon. This is the weapon we must use to break free from the stronghold of emotional eating. We'll spend the rest of the week learning how to use this weapon.

In closing, write the words of Jesus in John 8:31-32. This is a wonderful promise we can rely on as we go to God for help with emotional eating.

_____

_____

DAY 2

Our lesson today is a little longer than normal but it holds biblical truths that will set the foundation for the rest of the study. Let's begin by reading Romans 12:1-2:

Therefore I urge you, brethren, by the mercies of God, to present your bodies a living and holy sacrifice, acceptable to God, which is your spiritual service of worship. And do not be conformed to this world, but be transformed by the renewing of your mind, so that you may prove what the will of God is, that which is good and acceptable and perfect. NASB

What three things does Paul tell us to do in these verses?

1._____

2._____

3._____

How are we to be transformed?

_____

In this passage Paul tells us to present our bodies as a living sacrifice. The Greek word used for sacrifice is *thusia*. This word is also a root in the Greek word for the altar the Jewish people sacrificed their animals on. When Paul uses the word sacrifice here, he's not just talking about putting up with a little inconvenience. He's talking about giving up everything.

When I think of Christians making sacrifices, my first thoughts are of persecuted Christians living in countries hostile to the gospel. Our brothers and sisters in those countries endure hardships we can't even begin to imagine. The things we give up as Christians living in a free country seem small in comparison, but they're still sacrifices and they still please God.

Can you think of any sacrifices you've made for God?

_____

_____

Another interesting thing in Romans 12:1 is the use of the phrase "spiritual act of worship." The Greek word translated spiritual is *logikane*. The definition of *logikane* is "rational, belonging to the sphere of reason."

Presenting our bodies as a living sacrifice is a rational, thought-out process. It's not just saying, "Lord, I'll do whatever you want me to do," and then sitting back to wait for a feeling of what we should do.

Instead, it's taking a rational look at our lives. What sins need to go so we can better reflect His love to others? What activities need to go so we can put Him first in our lives? What thoughts need to go so we can keep our minds pure before Him?

Worshiping God like this involves sacrifice as we give up anything that gets in the way of serving Him. It's far easier to say, "Lord, just tell me what you want me to do and I'll do it. I'm willing to do anything."

When this is our focus, we can feel noble even though we're not really doing anything. After all, we're *willing* to do anything; we just don't know what God wants us to do yet.

This is another trick of Satan's—getting us to focus on searching for the specific thing God wants us to do while ignoring all the things He's already told us to do in His Word.

• How would it change your walk with God if you focused as much energy on doing the things God has already told you to do in the Bible as you do on trying to discover His individual will for your life?

_____

_____

Many people have been turned off by Christianity because of the things they see Christians doing. When they see Christians being judgmental, self-centered, impure, and unloving, they think, *Why would I want to be a Christian?* They might have those same characteristics themselves, but they feel like Christians should be different. After all, shouldn't Christians practice what they preach?

• How would you answer those critics of Christianity?

_____

_____

God calls us to be different, and He has empowered us to be different. It grieves

Him to see us living like the world and giving the old "oh, this is just my personality" excuse over and over again.

We also grieve. We feel badly about living defeated lives. We want to break free from our sin. We want to let go of our anger and worry and all the other emotions that trip us up. But we just can't seem to change no matter how hard we try.

What then can we do? How can we break out of this self-centered pattern to live the life God calls us to live? The answer is found in Romans 12:2: We are to be transformed by the renewing of our minds.

Paul tells us more about the renewing of the mind in Ephesians 4:22-24. Read the passage below and then do the following: Circle the words deceit and truth, and put a box around the phrases "lay aside the old self" and "put on the new self." Underline "be renewed in the spirit of your mind" and then answer the questions that follow.

That in reference to your former manner of life, you lay aside the old self, which is being corrupted in accordance with the lusts of deceit, and that you be renewed in the spirit of your mind, and put on the new self, which in the likeness of God has been created in righteousness and holiness of the truth.

NASB

What two things does Paul tell us to do before we put on the new self?

_____

_____

When we get dressed each day, we always take off the old before we put on the new. It wouldn't even cross our minds to put our clothes over our pajamas because it would make us look fat! Not to mention being very uncomfortable. We take off one outfit before we put on the next because life just works better that way.

It's the same way with our minds. They work better if we get rid of the old thoughts before we put on the new thoughts. I learned this lesson the hard way. When I became a Christian in junior high school, I already had a lot of thoughts going on, a lot of ungodly thoughts if truth be told.

As I read my Bible, I began to take on new thoughts. The problem was that I didn't get rid of the old thoughts. I lived like this for almost thirty years, experiencing some success in my walk with God, but mostly a lot of failure. He was a part of my life, a very good part, but He wasn't the center of my life.

It wasn't until I started renewing my mind on a regular basis that I began to experience growth in my character. I needed to get rid of those old thoughts in order for the new thoughts to take over. Paul calls this process "getting rid of the old self and replacing it with the new self."

What does Paul say is corrupting the old self?

_____

This is very interesting. The word *deceit* in the Greek is in the genitive case. This is the noun case of possession or belonging. For example, in the phrase "word of

God," *word* is in the genitive case. That means that the word belongs to God and comes from God. It's God's word. In the phrase "lusts of deceit," the lust belongs to the lie (deceit) and comes from the lie.

This is how it works in practice: The lies we believe create intense desires in us. Those intense desires (lusts) lead to corrupt, old-self behavior. We could show the relationship with this diagram.

Lies (Deceit) → Intense Desires (Lusts) → Corruption (Old Self)

In Ephesians 4:24, truth is also in the genitive case. From what you know about the genitive case, what is the relationship between truth and holiness in this verse?

_____

Isn't that interesting? The holiness belongs to and comes from the truth. We could show this relationship by the following diagram:

Truth → Right Desires or a Lack of Intense Wrong Desires → Holiness (New Self)

• Now look back at the two diagrams and read the Bible passage again. What will happen if you put on the truth without taking off the lie?

_____

_____

Truth gives us the right desires, but if we don't take off the lies before we put on the truth, then we'll still struggle with those wrong desires. It's *essential* to take off the old before we put on the new. If we don't, we'll struggle with those wrong desires for the rest of our lives.

• Can you think of any examples of people having wrong desires and actions because of the lies they believe?

_____

_____

Now let's tie this idea into our struggle with emotional eating. Just as lies cause wrong desires and actions in other areas of our lives, they do the same in the area of eating. The reason we overeat is because of the lies we believe.

Can you think of any lies you believe about life or food that make you want to eat too much?

_____

_____

One of the lies I used to believe was "I deserve a reward for doing hard things." This was a problem because I was a stay-at-home mom, and no one was rewarding me for the hard things I was doing. I solved the problem by rewarding myself with food.

This made it hard for me to lose weight and keep it off. That lie and others were creating such intense desires in me that I didn't have the self-control to follow my boundaries long-term. Sooner or later, I'd give up and go back to my old ways.

Now you might be thinking, "But is there anything wrong with rewarding yourself for a job? That doesn't sound like a lie to me." This is where Satan is so tricky. He's the master of partial truth.

Here's the whole truth: There is nothing wrong with rewarding ourselves for a difficult job, but it's not true that we *deserve* a reward. God never promised us an easy life. Instead He warned us that we would go through tough times. And He never said, "But after the hard times, you will deserve a treat."

Do you see how a lie can make us eat too much? It can also keep us from going to God for help. It seems like such a little thing—a bowl of ice cream after the kids go down for their naps, a bag of chips after work, a few doughnuts after tackling that big project—what's the big deal? But it actually is a big deal. Because we're forming a habit of depending on food for our emotional needs rather than God.

Let's go back to the "I deserve a treat when I do something hard" example. When that thought enters our minds, we have several choices. We can:

1. Try not to have a treat, even though we believe we deserve it.
2. Forget about the boundaries and eat that great treat.
3. Eat some carrots and celery instead.
4. Do something to take our minds off food.
5. Renew our minds: Take off the lies that make us break our boundaries and replace them with the truth that will set us free.

• What are the benefits of choosing the fifth option?

_____

_____

This is what the fifth option looks like: Every time we think, "I deserve a treat," we tell ourselves, "No, God said that life would be hard. Suffering is to be expected, and I'm not even suffering compared to many people in the world," or something else along those lines.

If we do this *every time* that lie pops into our minds, one day we'll hear the truth as soon as we hear the lie. Eventually, we won't even hear the lie. And when that day comes, we'll do something hard, and we won't feel like rewarding ourselves with a treat.

This may seem simplistic, but it's not easy. You may renew your mind today and believe the exact same lie tomorrow. To experience victory, you'll have to keep renewing your mind every time you hear the lie until you believe the truth at the core level. You'll know this has happened when your desires change.

DAY 3

Today, I'd like to revisit the subject of strongholds that we discussed briefly in the introduction. If you haven't read the introduction yet, go back and read it, as it ties into today's lesson.

In the Old Testament a stronghold was a physical place that people went to for protection, usually an actual fortress. Because the strongholds were built to withstand attack, they were difficult to tear down. They felt like safe places.

David also used the word stronghold in the spiritual sense to refer to God. In Psalm 37:39 David said, "The salvation of the righteous comes from the Lord; He is their stronghold in time of trouble."

God was David's stronghold, and He wants to be our stronghold. He wants us to come to Him for refuge when life gets hard. But that's not always our first impulse, is it?

Instead, we head for other refuges. These refuges *feel* safe. They offer comfort, pleasure, security, and a way to escape. They're easy to go to, but they soon become hard to leave. What starts as a refuge ends as a stronghold. And strongholds are hard to tear down.

• In what way has food been a refuge for you, either now or in the past? Has it become a stronghold in your life?

_____

_____

_____

Let's see what Paul has to say about strongholds in 2 Corinthians 10:3-5.

For though we live in the world, we do not wage war as the world does. The weapons we fight with are not the weapons of the world. On the contrary, they have divine power to demolish strongholds. We demolish arguments and every pretension that sets itself up against the knowledge of God, and we take captive every thought to make it obedient to Christ.

What are two characteristics of the weapons we're supposed to use against strongholds?

1. _____

2. _____

List some divinely powerful weapons you could use in your battle against the stronghold of emotional eating.

_____

_____

List some weapons of the world you might use in your battle against the stronghold of emotional eating.

_____

- In your past efforts to lose weight, have you been using divinely powerful weapons or weapons of the world? How have those weapons worked?

_____

_____

Do you see our problem? We've been using the wrong weapons. If food is a stronghold for us, then we need to use weapons with divine power to break strongholds. Diet, exercise, and lifelong boundaries are all tools we can use, but they aren't powerful enough to tear down strongholds.

The literal Greek translation of the phrase "divine power" is *powerful in God*. God releases His power to change our lives through these weapons. Note that He's releasing the power to get rid of the stronghold, not to make us skinny.

Emotional eating may be a stronghold, but wanting to look good in the eyes of the world may also be a stronghold. Complicated, isn't it? God's not going to release His power just so we can lose weight and look good. He wants us to see ourselves through *His* eyes and seek His approval.

Does this mean that if your main purpose for this study is to lose weight, that God isn't going to help? No, not at all. That's probably how most of us start out. In fact, you could say we're lucky to have a stronghold that isn't approved of by society. It motivates us to work on it.

Hopefully, though, you'll shift your focus at some point in the study. The act of emotional eating is a much bigger problem than the extra pounds you carry. God adores you. He loves you just the way you are, at the weight you are. But He wants to be first in your life.

This study will help you become aware of the reasons you eat. As you uncover the lies that make you want to overeat and replace those lies with the truth, the desire to eat will lose its grip on you. As food takes its rightful place as the answer to hunger and not the answer to life's problems, you'll begin to lose weight.

So it's all kind of exciting, isn't it? Growing in our relationship with God, getting rid of strongholds, and losing some weight on the side. Let's look at those divinely powerful weapons and get started!

Read 2 Corinthians 10:3-5 once more. What two things does Paul tell us to do in 2 Corinthians 10:5?

1._____

_____

2._____

Does this sound familiar? It reminds me of the process of renewing our minds. First you destroy the wrong thinking, and second, you take your thoughts captive to Christ. Let's explore the wrong thinking part of this verse a little more. The word arguments in verse 5 is the Greek word *logismos*. It can also be translated reasoning. We are to demolish any reasonings that set themselves up against the knowledge of God.

Here's an example of a reasoning: I might believe that a treat will make me feel better. This isn't a thought that just popped into my head one day. Instead, I came to believe it through many times when a treat actually did make me feel better.

Think of growing up. A little kid falls down and scrapes her knee. What does her mom say? "Why don't we go have a cookie? That will make you feel better." Mom's motive is a noble one. She wants to make the little girl forget about her knee. She doesn't realize that she's planting the seeds of a lie into her daughter's mind.

You see, the child really will feel better after she eats the cookie because it doesn't take that long to make a scraped knee feel better. The little girl doesn't know that, though. Instead, she's beginning to believe the lie that sweets make her feel better.

The next thing Paul tells us to do in 2 Corinthians 10:5 is to take our thoughts captive to Christ. The Greek word for "take captive" has the idea of taking someone captive as a prisoner. Is a prisoner free to do what he pleases? No, of course not. His guard controls his every move.

In like manner, we need to control our thoughts, not just letting them run amok in our minds, but controlling them like a guard controls his prisoners. We do that by examining our thoughts to see if we're believing any lies.

Why don't we try that right now? I'm going to list some common beliefs about food, and I want you to circle the ones you believe—not at the intellectual level, but at the gut feeling level, your first reaction.

When you're through, look at each of the sentences you've circled and ask, "Is this really true?" The answer to that question should be no! Remember, Satan is the master of the partial truth. Some of them might be partly true, but none of them are completely true. Write the *full* truth below each sentence. If you need help, check out the list in Appendix A in the back of the book. I'll do the first two for you, and you can do the rest.

Lies That Keep Us From Losing Weight

1. I'll start being faithful to my boundaries tomorrow. (As you know, this is usually said to justify eating something really great tonight!)

Truth: *If past experience is any indication, there is about a 5% chance that I'll follow my boundaries tomorrow if I break them today. My best chance of being faithful tomorrow is to be faithful today.*

2. Eating is fun.

Truth: *Eating a reasonable amount is fun. Eating too much is not fun. It makes me feel uncomfortable, lethargic, and unhappy. It also makes me gain weight, which isn't fun.*

3. I can't stick to my boundaries. I have no self-control.

4. Just one little bite won't hurt.

5. I don't know when I'll get _____ again. I better eat it now.

6. I've been following my boundaries perfectly for *two weeks* and haven't lost anything. These boundaries don't work.

7. I already broke my boundaries. I might as well eat _____.

8. I've been so good at following my boundaries that I deserve a treat.

9. Eating will make me feel better.

10. Maybe I'll sleep better if I have something to eat.

11. It's only dough. It's hardly even a cookie.

12. I want it (and that's a good reason to have it).

13. I'm on vacation (at a party, etc.). It's okay to eat.

14. I'll feel more like doing _____ if I have something to eat first.

15. It will go to waste if I don't eat it.

16. I don't eat that much. I just have a low metabolism. (Note: This may be true.)

17. I'm so tired. Maybe a treat will perk me up a little bit.

18. This is so good that I should have another piece.

19. I gained _____ pounds this weekend.

20. I will never be able to lose weight and keep it off.

How did you do? These are the lies you believe that make you want to break your boundaries. If you were to stop believing them, you wouldn't feel like eating in those situations anymore. Let me encourage you by saying that I used to believe all but one of those lies. There are only a few I still struggle with, and that's because I haven't applied the truth often enough when the lie comes into my mind.

As I got rid of the lies one by one, my behavior began to change. The truth started coming to my mind automatically, and when that happened, I no longer felt like eating for the wrong reasons. Because I didn't *feel* like eating, I didn't. The key to behavior change is to replace lies with truth at the core of your being. The rest of the week will be devoted to that practice.

DAY 4

Then you will know the truth, and the truth will set you free. John 8:32

Today we'll begin using divine weapons in our battle against the stronghold of emotional eating. We'll use the truth in two different ways. The first is a process I call truth journaling, which is a practical way to bring thoughts captive to the truth. The second is the practice of Scripture prayers and memorization, which we'll cover tomorrow.

Before we look at truth journaling, let's study John 8:31-34. Who is Jesus talking to in this passage?

_____

These verses are about sanctification, not salvation. Jesus was talking to believers. In verses 31-32 He mentions three things that will happen to those who abide in His Word. What are they?

1._____

2._____

3._____

This is important. These things don't happen to us automatically by believing in

Jesus. They happen to us by abiding in His Word. Abiding in the Word is different than just reading the Word. Instead, we're bringing it into our lives, thinking about it during the day, and using it to show us how to live life. It's a back-and-forth conversation between God, His Word, and us as we walk through life.

Truth journaling is a tool that can help you talk through life with God. It's a practical way to carry your thoughts captive to the truth. We'll use truth journaling throughout this book to go to God for help with our emotions, but let's begin by taking a look at how truth journaling can help with emotional eating.

There are two different ways you can journal. First, you can look at the things you believe that make you think eating is a good response to your negative emotions. Second, you can look at the things you believe that are creating those negative emotions.

For example, if you eat when you're worried, you can either learn not to eat when you're worried (the first journaling method), or you can learn how to get rid of your worry (the second journaling method). In the first case, you'll still have the worry; you're just realizing that food isn't the answer. In the second case, you're actually getting rid of the worry.

You see, not only do we believe lies that make us eat, we also believe lies that make us worry and lies that make us angry and lies that make us emotionally distraught in other ways. If we replace those lies with the truth, our negative emotions will fade away. If the negative emotion is giving us the desire to eat, then the urge to eat will usually disappear with the negative emotion.

How to Truth Journal

The challenge is first to learn *how* to truth journal and second to take the time to truth journal. The sooner you journal after each eating mishap, the easier it will be to remember what you were thinking before you ate.

Journaling right away will also help you eat less. For example, have you ever broken your boundaries early in the day and thought, "Oh well, I already blew it, I might as well give up and start again tomorrow"?

This is a natural reaction, but it's based on a lie. In reality, the sooner you stop the better. Journaling right away will focus your mind on the truth, which will change your desires and actions.

When you journal, don't worry about organizing and analyzing your thoughts before you write. Just spill them out on the pages of your journal. Then look at each sentence, one at a time, to see if it's a lie or a truth, and replace any lies with truth.

If you're having trouble coming up with the truth, ask yourself, "What would God say about this sentence? Does He think it's the truth?" Many times the truth will come in the form of a Bible verse or a biblical principle, but not always. Sometimes it will just be a practical truth. Remember, though, that it will never go *against* Scripture.

The more often you journal, the faster you'll change. I began truth journaling seven years ago, and I can't tell you how much God has used it to change my life. I hope that you'll make the effort to learn and practice this discipline.

Let's look at some examples of truth journaling to see how it works. Read through them now and then refer back to these examples later as you learn how to truth journal on your own.

Journaling Method #1: Journaling about Food

You can see how this type of journaling works by looking at a journal entry I made just the other night. First let me give you some background. I frequently wake up in the middle of the night to work on this Bible study. I home school my three kids (the fourth is off at college) so the middle of the night is a good time to think and write without getting interrupted. This was one of those middle of the night sessions.

My current boundaries are three meals and one snack a day. Also, I'm not eating sweets right now because I'm trying to find the easiest way to lose weight on the boundary system.

Here's the situation: I didn't feel like writing, so I thought, *I know, I'll have a little bowl of granola first, then I'll write.* Then I ate my granola. I was actually craving a sweet but settled for the next best thing since I was off sweets. I wasn't hungry, just procrastinating. Here's what I wrote after the fact. Notice I'm analyzing what my thoughts were *before* I ate.

I think I'll eat a bowl of granola; that would be a treat. I deserve one since writing this Bible study is so hard, plus I can't have sweets so at least granola would be something kind of good. I just won't have a snack tomorrow, so I can still eat this, and it won't hurt me.

Do you see how I'm just throwing my thoughts out there without taking the time to organize them or make them sound good? Since the goal of journaling is to carry each thought captive to the truth, it's important to write down your thoughts without censoring them. Then examine each thought individually to see if it's a lie.

This is key. Our tendency is to look at the whole picture, bring in the past, and get bogged down in a negative thought cycle. We can prevent that by looking at our thoughts, one at a time, and bringing each thought captive to the truth.

So, back to my example, the next thing you do is number your thoughts. Don't rewrite the sentences. Just pencil in little numbers in front of each sentence. This is what it will look like:

1. I think I'll eat a bowl of granola; that would be a treat. 2. I deserve one since writing this Bible study is so hard. 3. Plus I can't have sweets so at least granola would be something kind of good. 4. I just won't have a snack tomorrow, so I can still eat this, and it won't hurt me.

Next I go through each sentence one at a time to determine the truth. Let me show you what I wrote in my journal that night. I'll write each sentence with its corresponding truth so it will be easier to follow.

1. I think I'll eat a bowl of granola; that would be a treat.

Truth: It won't be a treat because I'm not even in the mood for granola. I'm more in the mood for ice cream.

2. I deserve a treat since writing this Bible study is so hard.

Truth: Yes, my life is hard, but having a treat will keep me from going to God and

28

growing. I'd rather have character development than five minutes of granola.

3. Plus I can't have sweets so at least granola would be something kind of good.

Truth: First, I can have sweets if I want. I'm choosing not to for the greater good. Also, the granola wasn't that great since I wasn't in the mood for it.

4. I just won't have a snack tomorrow, so I can still eat this, and it won't hurt me.

Truth: Actually there's a good chance that I'll feel deprived tomorrow when I can't have a snack. This might tempt me to eat outside my boundaries and have a snack anyway, which would make me feel discouraged and want to eat more. So there's a good chance it will hurt me.

Do you see how it works? As I wrote the truth down, I began to *believe* the truth. The character development part really got to me. Life is hard at times. But God uses hard times for good when we go to Him for help.

Journaling helped me realize the whole truth of the situation. It was no longer just, "I want a sweet and I'm deprived—poor me." Instead, I saw the wisdom of not having a treat.

The bottom line was that the Bible study was still going to be there to write after I finished my granola. I only delayed it by five minutes. Did the granola make it easier to write? No, not at all. It just made it easier to break my boundaries the next time I didn't feel like writing.

Note: It took me more than two years to write this Bible study, so you'll notice that my boundaries change from time to time throughout the book. Shortly after I wrote this, I changed my boundaries to three meals and two snacks, and currently my boundaries are three meals and no snacks unless I'm hungry.

Journaling Method #2: Journaling about Emotions

To illustrate this method of journaling, I'll use the same situation but approach it from a different angle. Instead of looking at the beliefs that were making me want to eat, we'll look at the beliefs that were causing the *emotions* that were making me want to eat. Let me explain.

Before I had the granola, I was dreading writing the Bible study. I've been feeling overwhelmed by it lately since I'm teaching my first class next week and I've had to completely rewrite this chapter, in addition to editing all of the other chapters. These feelings were the reasons I wanted to have a treat in the first place. If I'd gotten up in the middle of the night to read a novel, I wouldn't have felt like eating. Let me try journaling this for you.

I am tired of writing this study. I have no idea how to write this chapter. It's too hard. I can't do it.

Again, the first thing I would do is number the sentences. It would look like this:

1. I am tired of writing this study. 2. I have no idea how to write this chapter. 3. It's too hard. 4. I can't do it.

Next, I would look at each sentence, one at a time, and write the truth for it. This is how the entry would look in my journal:

1. True (Note: This is actually a feeling, not a belief, so you can't really say much about it.) *2. True 3. It is hard, but not too hard. I can do hard things.* (How many times have I said that to my kids?) *Also, I can do all things through Him who strengthens me. 4. I can't do it easily. But I can do it. I can't do it perfectly. But I can do it. If God really wants me to write this study, then He will show me how to do it. All I have to do is put in the time.*

If I had journaled like this before I ate the granola, I wouldn't have felt like eating the granola anymore—honestly. You will be amazed at how this works. The truth really does set you free. My dread of writing would also have disappeared.

You see, my real problem was perfectionism, but I didn't know that until I journaled. Subconsciously, I was feeling like my Bible study had to be perfect. That's why I dreaded writing it. When I realized I didn't *have* to make it perfect and only needed to obey God, I began to feel better right away.

A person who doesn't struggle with perfectionism and doesn't expect life to be easy would write a whole different journal entry than I would write. That's what's so great about truth journaling. We each have our own set of lies to deal with, and truth journaling helps us discover those lies.

Assignment

For the next two weeks, I'd like you to try truth journaling once a day. Remember, this is different than regular journaling. You're not just writing your thoughts and feelings to get them out of your system. You're writing them down so you can bring them captive to the truth.

If you eat outside your boundaries, try to journal that situation. If you need help discovering the lies that make you eat, look for ideas in Appendix A. If you're experiencing a negative emotion, try journaling that. Don't get discouraged if you don't come to peace right away after journaling. It's difficult to learn how to journal emotions well. It will become easier as we study each individual emotion. I'll provide a space for you to truth journal at the end of each lesson. Why don't you try your first entry now?

Truth Journal

*Situation*_____

*Emotion*_____

*Belief*_____

_____

_____

*Truth*_____

_____

_____

_____

How did you do? Easier than you thought? Harder than you thought? Keep trying it at least once a day, and you'll soon become proficient at it. After a few weeks of journaling, you may begin to notice patterns.

For instance, when I first started journaling for emotional eating, I noticed that I felt like I deserved a treat after doing something really stressful or unpleasant. If I was expecting a stressful event, I learned to save my snack so that I could have it after the event was over.

This practice kept me from breaking my boundaries. Eventually the truth set me free from that belief and I no longer felt the urge to eat in that situation. Once my beliefs changed, I went back to having my snack whenever I felt like having it.

As you noticed in today's journaling examples, I still have the urge to eat to avoid certain situations. However, I'm losing my desire to eat when the situation is over. I'm beginning to see that I don't deserve a treat whenever I do something unpleasant.

God is using the *truth*—not self-control—to change my behavior. I came to believe the truth through many journaling opportunities created by a *lack* of self-control.

As we get into the chapters on the emotions, your journal entries will become more personal so you may want to have a separate journal. If you're worried about others seeing what you wrote, write your entry on a piece of paper that you can throw away after you're through writing. Truth journaling takes time, but it's well worth the effort!

DAY 5

Have you ever thought about what a gift the Bible is? One of the gifts in the Bible is the account of how Jesus handled temptation. What better way to find out how we should deal with it than to see how Jesus dealt with it? Let's look at the story of His temptation in Luke 4:1-13.

• Read and record some of the things you observe in these verses about the way Jesus dealt with temptation.

_____

_____

_____

Did you notice how Jesus answered each temptation? There was no discussion, no rationalization, no checking His feelings to see what He *felt* like doing. Instead, each time Satan gave Jesus a temptation, Jesus gave Satan a Bible verse. In fact, in these 13 verses, only three sentences belong to Jesus. And each sentence is a direct quote from Scripture. Jesus answered temptation with the truth.

Hebrews 4:15 is another verse that gives us hope when it comes to temptation. What three things does this verse say about Jesus and temptation?

1. _____

2. _____

3. _____

Isn't it a comfort to know that Jesus understands our weakness? He doesn't condemn us. He understands what we're going through because He's gone through it too. The only difference is that Jesus never gave in. He answered temptation with the Word of God, and He never sinned.

Jesus had the truth in His heart and on the tip of His tongue, ready to answer Satan the moment He was tempted. If Jesus used Scripture to withstand temptation, shouldn't we be doing the same thing? We need to hide His Word in our hearts so it's ready to use the moment we're attacked.

Today I'd like you to prepare a little battle book. I've provided you with some Bible verses you can use when you experience negative emotions. Choose some passages that you think will help you in your moment of temptation and jot them down someplace where you'll be able to easily find them. I purchased a spiral index card book and wrote one verse on each card.

Use these verses to pray through when you're tempted. Beth Moore has an excellent book on praying Scripture called "Praying God's Word" that you may like to use as another resource.

Here's an example of a prayer I could have prayed the other night when I was struggling with procrastination. The prayer is based on Philippians 4:13, "I can do all things through Him who gives me strength."

Lord, you say I can do all things through you, but I feel like this is something I can't do. I know I can't do it perfectly, yet I believe that you've called me to do it. I'm thankful that you are a God who doesn't demand perfection and only asks for a willing heart. Please strengthen me, Lord. Help me to look at your strength and not my own weakness. Please help me not to procrastinate. Thank You Lord that you are a God that loves me so well. I submit myself to your will.

Write your prayers in your journal or pray silently as you look at the Scripture. You could also memorize the verse and meditate on its meaning. Putting God's word in your heart will make it easy to retrieve, and it will be there when you need it in moments of temptation.

I often take my Bible verse notebook with me when I go on walks, when I garden, when I work around the house, and when I go on long car trips. I have my daily quiet times in the morning and sometimes use my verse notebook in the afternoon for prayer and meditation.

Please take the time now to write some verses down and try praying through some of them. This is not an exhaustive list, but hopefully you'll find some verses to help.

Bible Verses

Anger/Resentment Psalm 37:8, Proverbs 14:29-30, Matthew 5:43-44, Matthew 7:1-5, Romans 12:19-21, 1 Corinthians 13, James 1:19-21, Ephesians 4:26-27, Colossians 3:12-17

Anxiety/Worry Psalm 138:7-8, John 14:27, Matthew 6:25-34, Philippians 4:19, Philippians 4:4-7

Depression Psalm 42:5-6, Lamentations 3, 1 Thessalonians 5:16-19

Desire to Eat Nehemiah 2:17-20, Psalm 25:15, 1 Corinthians 10:13-14, 2 Corinthians 10:3-6, Galatians 6:9, Hebrews 2:18, 10:36, 2 Thessalonians 3:3

Failure/Discouragement 2 Chronicles 20:12,15, Isaiah 43:18-19, Isaiah 40:28-31, James 1:2-5,12, Psalm 42:5-6, Matthew 11:28-30, 2 Corinthians 4:8-9, 12:9, Hebrews 4:14-16, 12:1-13, John 16:33, Galatians 6:9

Fear Psalm 27:1-8, Psalm 71, Proverbs 30:5, 2 Chronicles 20:1-4,12-30, Hebrews 13:5-6

Loneliness Psalm 25:1, 16-18, Psalm 57:1-3, Psalm 61:1-5, Psalm 62:1-2, Psalm 63

Perfectionism Matthew 6:19-21, 24, 33-34, Matthew 11:28-30, Luke 6:36-37, Galatians 1:10, Colossians 3:1-3

Procrastination Proverbs 13:4, Proverbs 15:19, Matthew 19:26, 2 Corinthians 12:9, Galatians 6:9, Philippians 4:13, Colossians 3:23-24, Hebrews 10:36

Stress Proverbs 3:5-6, Matthew 6:33, Matthew 22:36-39, 2 Corinthians 12:9-10, Philippians 4:13

Unhappiness/Discontent Psalm 68:19-20, Psalm 138, Philippians 3:7-14, 4:4, 8-13, 19, 1 Timothy 6:6-12, 1 John 2:15-17

God's Word is powerful to bring about change in our lives. On page 53, I've listed some verses that will help you in your struggle with emotional eating. If you pray through this list once or twice a day, you'll be amazed at how God will use His Word to change your attitude. Why don't you try praying through some of those verses right now? Also, don't forget your journaling for the day!

Truth Journal

Situation_____

Emotion_____

Belief_____

_____

_____

_____

Truth_____

_____

_____

_____

_____

_____

_____

Note: On page 166 I've included a chart you can use for truth journaling if you'd rather use that then a journal. Just copy it off and store the pages in a ring binder. If you journal every time you break your boundaries, you'll soon discover the lies you believe that are making you break your boundaries. The more often you replace the lies with the truth, the sooner you'll believe the truth. Once you believe the truth, you will lose your desire to overeat.

Trials

Have you ever felt that life is just too hard? Too many problems? Too many trials? We know that God uses trials for our good, but that doesn't necessarily make it easy to accept them, does it? Often our reaction is negative. "What can I do to get out of this?" we ask, or "What can I do to make the pain go away?" Too often the answer is "I know. I'll have some ice cream."

God wants to bring good things out of the trials we go through, but when we use food to escape, we miss out on all He's trying to teach us. This week we'll discuss God's purposes for trials and how we can respond to them in a way that will help us be more like Him.

DAY 1

Can you think of any trials in your life that are worse than wandering in a desert for forty years? Probably not! The Israelites suffered many hardships in the desert because they chose to rely on their own strength rather than trusting in God.

You remember the story. God had miraculously delivered the Israelites from slavery and brought them out of Egypt. He was ready to bring them into the Promised Land, but first He wanted Moses to send twelve men into Canaan to spy out the land.

God wasn't sending the men to see *if* they could take the country. He had already told the Israelites He was going to give it to them (Numbers 13:1-2). The passage doesn't say why God asked them to spy out Canaan. Maybe He wanted them to be familiar with the territory before they took it over. Maybe He wanted them to see what a great gift He was giving them. And maybe He was testing them to see if they would trust Him. We don't know.

What we do know is that Moses obeyed God. He sent one man from each tribe, and they explored the land for forty days. They came back with a mixed report. Yes, the land was wonderful, but there was a problem. The cities were large and well fortified—and there were some really huge people living there. There was *no way* the Israelites were strong enough to conquer those people.

Two of the spies, Joshua and Caleb, told the people not to worry. They knew that God had promised them the land, and they knew God was all-powerful. He would give them victory.

The other ten spies weren't so confident. Instead of focusing on God's strength, they focused on their own weakness. And there was no way they could conquer that land. Their advice? Go back to Egypt where life was comfortable and safe. The people agreed. In fact, they were trying to decide who should lead them back to Egypt when God intervened.

He punished the Israelites by telling them that they would never see the Promised Land. Instead they would wander the desert for forty years. He would use that time to prepare the hearts of their children so they would trust in God and possess the new land.

Well, the Israelites did spend the next forty years in the desert, and God used that time for His purposes. Deuteronomy 8 is a wonderful chapter that talks about God's reasons for letting them sojourn so long in a set of circumstances they weren't crazy about. As you read this chapter, think of your own life. Are you going through some things that aren't pleasant? Could it be that God has a purpose for you in that suffering? Let's look at the reasons He gives for allowing the Israelites to suffer.

Read Deuteronomy 8 and list God's purposes for letting the Israelites wander the desert for 40 years.

8:2_____

8:3_____

8:5-6_____

8:11-14_____

8:7,16_____

8:17-18_____

• Now look back over the things you wrote, thinking about one of your own trials. Do you suppose God may be trying to accomplish something in your life through your struggles? List below any purposes you think God may have for allowing you to suffer.

_____

_____

It was God's intention all along to bring the children of the Israelites to the Promised Land, but He needed to prepare them to enter the Promised Land first—and that preparation involved some suffering.

God also has a purpose for the struggles you and I go through. He wants to use our trials to change us in ways we *need* to change, but too often we turn to food instead for escape and comfort. When we turn to food instead of Him, we miss out on some of the good things He wants to give us.

In your journaling today, why don't you record some of the beliefs you've had about a trial in your life? Use the Deuteronomy 8 passage for help in replacing lies with truth.

Truth Journal

*Situation*_____

*Emotion*_____

*Belief*_____

_____

_____

_____

*Truth*_____

_____

_____

_____

_____

DAY 2

Let me ask you something. What is your natural attitude toward suffering? Do you think "Well, that's not surprising; everyone has to suffer now and then," or is it more like "This isn't fair! Why do I have to go through so much when my friends have the easy life?"

We are blessed to live in a wealthy country. We have nice houses, good food, and excellent health care. While living in such bounty is pleasant, it can also be dangerous to our walk with God.

Because we're so accustomed to being able to fix all of our problems, we begin to think that we deserve to have every problem fixed. Then when things go wrong, as they inevitably do, we're upset because our lives are so hard. We haven't learned how to accept and even *expect* suffering as part of life.

Don't get me wrong—I'm not saying we can't work to improve our situations in life. We just need to learn that it's not our God-given right to have everything perfect and easy. In fact, God doesn't even want everything to be perfect and easy in our lives. He uses hard things to make us grow.

James talks about this in James 1:2-17. Read through this passage once and then we'll look at it verse by verse. What does verse 2 say that our attitude should be toward trials?

_____

Paul tells us to count it all joy when we encounter trials. The Greek word for *count* is interesting. The noun form of the word is always translated governor, ruler or prince. The idea behind the word is that we are supposed to be in charge of (govern) how we view trials. We can either think of them as horrible things that we don't deserve, or we can think of them as necessary things that God uses to shape and develop our character.

If our lives are focused on fun and comfort, then trials are to be avoided at all costs. If our lives are focused on living for God, then trials are opportunities for growth. We may not *feel* joyful about them, but we "count it all joy" because we know God uses them for our good.

Now let's look at verse 3. What does the testing of our faith produce?

_____

The Greek word for perseverance (your translation may say endurance or steadfastness) is *hupomone*. This word is made up of two smaller words. *Hupo* means under and *mone* means abide. So the literal translation would be "to abide under."

Ancient Greeks used this word to refer to an active enduring of a trial rather than a passive waiting. The person who was going through the trial had a job to perform. Think of running a marathon as opposed to waiting in a doctor's office.

In a spiritual sense, *hupomone* is actively enduring the trial, but doing it under the shelter of God's protection. I would say, "Yes, this is difficult, but I'll lean on the Lord and together we'll fight this battle. I will not give up!" Contrast that with the attitude of someone saying, "I can't stand all this suffering. I guess I'll put up with it, but I don't have to like it."

Do you see the difference? Active perseverance produces maturity, but passive resignation only produces dissatisfaction. The key is in the refuge.

If God is my refuge, it will be easier to actively persevere and to "count it all joy" during a trial. When food is my refuge, it's more common to have a bad attitude, become discouraged, and give up.

In verse 12, who is blessed?

_____

This is significant. It's not the person who *goes through* the trial that's blessed. It's the person who *perseveres* through the trial. That would be the person who abides under God's care. We are misled when we think that trials in and of themselves make us stronger or more like Christ. They only do that if we handle them God's way. If we handle them *our* way—by escaping or complaining or eating or dwelling on how unfair life is—then they're more likely to produce anger, discontentment, hopelessness, or some other negative emotion.

What is the outcome of "abiding under" or perseverance? (James 1:4)

_____

We could view our trials as a character training school. In order to learn the lessons God wants us to learn, we need to submit to instruction and do what the Teacher asks us to do. That's not always fun. But the change in our character and the growth in our relationship with God will be more than worth it.

Verses 5-8 don't really seem to fit in here at first glance. Why do you think James shifts to asking God for wisdom all of a sudden? And what is he asking wisdom for?

_____

_____

We need to ask God for wisdom to know how to handle trials. Especially if we usually handle them by eating. We can also ask Him what He's trying to teach us through the trial. Our prayer should be, not to escape the difficult situation, but to glorify Him in all that we do.

That doesn't mean we can't ask Him to take away the trial. He's our Father. We can ask Him for anything. But we need to be willing to accept "no" for an answer. If He doesn't take away the trial, then we need to trust Him and not become double-minded people who question whether or not God knows what He's doing. He can bring good out of anything. We need to believe that.

Abiding in God during a trial is difficult, but it leads to character development and joy. Eating is easy, but it only brings momentary relief. It doesn't change our character, and it doesn't lead to joy.

Now let's skip down to verses 13-15. How are we tempted?

_____

The Greek word for tempt in these verses is *peirazo*. It's the verb form of the word that's usually translated *trial* in verse 2. When we look at these verses a little more closely, we'll see how the words trial and tempt are connected and why translators might use them interchangeably.

Notice it says that we are tempted by our own lusts. Often our sinful desires cause us to sin and the consequence of that sin becomes a trial in our lives.

• List some examples of sins that produce trials. (Can you think of any sins that *don't* produce trials?)

_____

_____

Giving into temptation often produces a trial in our lives. If we give in to the temptation of overeating too often, then we have the trial of being overweight. If we give into the temptation of procrastination, we'll have the trial of rushing around at the last minute to get things done.

• Just as giving into temptation can lead to trials, trials can lead us into temptation. Can you think of any examples of this?

_____

All of us have probably felt the temptation to overeat because of a trial in our lives. God isn't the one tempting us. He wants us to live a sin-free life. But He also doesn't fix everything when we mess up.

Think of a kid who forgets to bring his homework to school every day. If his mom always drives it over for him, the child won't learn responsibility. So she lets him suffer the consequences of his actions, hoping that he'll learn from his mistakes and become more responsible. Now she doesn't *make* him forget his homework in order to teach him a lesson. She just uses his own mistake and doesn't fix the problem for him.

How do you think James 1:19-20 ties in with the discussion on trials?

_____

Are you ever tempted to become angry when things don't go your way? If we want trials to produce righteousness in our lives, we have to give up our "rights" and humble ourselves. We don't deserve a trouble-free life.

God can teach us so much more when our hearts are submissive. When we become angry and turn to food for an escape, we miss what He's trying to teach us through that difficult situation in our lives.

That's why it's so important to follow our boundaries. If we can't eat when we're frustrated, we'll have to learn a new way of dealing with our problems. My friend, make sure that the "new way" is God.

You will be tempted at this stage to introduce another less fattening way of escape. Other forms of recreation may help you lose weight, but they won't help you gain victory over sin—and they could create another stronghold in your life. God is the only worthwhile refuge. The other refuges may be easier to go to, but they won't bring lasting peace. What they bring is immediate gratification and lasting bondage.

In closing, please paraphrase Hebrews 2:18 on the lines below.

_____

_____

Truth Journal

*Situation*_____

*Emotion*_____

*Belief*_____

_____

_____

*Truth*_____

_____

_____

_____

_____

_____

DAY 3

Yesterday we looked at one source of trials, that of our own sin. At least with a trial brought on by our own sin, we can say, "Well, I deserved that." Unfortunately, sometimes we have to endure trials based on the sins of others. Those aren't as easy to accept. We're inclined to say, "I don't deserve that!" and focus our attentions on blaming and being angry with the other person. Finally, we have trials that aren't based on sin at all, such as a trial due to an illness or a serious disease.

No matter what the origin of the trial, our response should be the same—to persevere and turn to God for help. You know as well as I do, though, that we don't always take that option.

Let's look at a real-life situation to see what other options we might take. We'll peek in on a normal day in the life of Mary and Bill. They have two kids and they both work full-time. After work, Mary makes dinner while Bill reads the newspaper. They all have dinner together and then Mary spends the rest of the evening doing the dishes, washing clothes, and helping the kids with their homework while Bill spends the rest of the evening watching television.

Do you think Mary feels like she's experiencing a trial when she looks at her life and compares it to Bill's life? I'll bet she does!

Imagine that Mary has asked Bill for help many times, without result. Usually Bill will say something like, "Okay, as soon as the show's over." But then another show starts, and he never quite gets around to doing anything.

• Is this trial a result of Mary's sin or Bill's sin? Explain.

_____

• Does Mary have a right to have Bill help her? What do you think Jesus would say?

_____

This is tricky, isn't it? I think we'd all agree that Mary has a right to have Bill help her. But what does Paul tell us to do in Philippians 2:1-8 and 1 John 3:16?

_____

_____

• What do you think that would look like in this situation?

_____

_____

Sometimes the Bible is so radical, we think, *What???? God wants us to do that???* But here's the interesting thing: The Bible works. When we do what it says with our heart as well as our behavior, we experience the fruit of the Spirit (Galatians 5:22-23). And one of those fruits is joy.

But of course doing what the Bible says with both our behavior and heart is not our natural reaction! Just think of how you'd feel if you were Mary. Would you be saying, "Oh, I just need to love and accept Bill as he is"? Or would you be saying, "There is no way I can be happy unless Bill changes"? I think most of us would be saying the latter.

At that point, we usually make one of two mistakes: Either we keep trying to change a person who isn't willing to change and get frustrated in the process, or we spend all of our time obsessing about the life that we *should* be having.

Day after day we think, *If only Bill would get off the couch and help around the house, then I would be happy*, or *If only Bill would get off the couch, then I could respect him*. Or *If only Bill would get off the couch, then I wouldn't be so stressed out.*

We waste our time and energy thinking about a life that doesn't exist. Bill has shown time after time that he's not willing to get off the couch. Unless he starts going to God for help with his problem of selfishness, there's not a lot of hope that he'll change.

Mary at this point has a choice. Does she cling to her "rights" and continue to be angry with Bill over his refusal to change his ways? Does she passively endure the trial, disgusted with Bill, but putting up with him anyway? Does she dump Bill and look for a husband who will help around the house?

Or does she lay down her rights in order to love Bill and her children well, actively persevering, going to God for refuge, and allowing her own character to be transformed through her suffering?

Real-Life Options

Sometimes in a situation like this it helps to look at our real-life options. Remember, changing Bill isn't an option for Mary. Only Bill can change Bill, and in reality, probably only God can change Bill.

So what are Mary's real-life options? Let's look at them and see how each option would affect 1) Mary's personal happiness, 2) Mary's relationship with God, and 3) the likelihood of changing Bill.

It would also be important to know how each of Mary's options would affect her children, but we'll leave that out of this example since we're mainly focusing on her frustration with Bill.

Option 1 *Divorce Bill.* I include divorce as an option only because it is an option. Since it might be a real temptation for Mary in this situation, I think it would be helpful to evaluate it.

Let's begin with the first question: Would divorce make Mary happy? Hard to say. She'd still have all that work to do, and she'd still have to deal with Bill's irresponsibility since they'd continue to share parenting duties. She'd probably be more stressed financially since they'd now have to support two households on the same income. And she'd also have to go through all the pain of divorce, including the pain of watching her kids go through the divorce. Would it make her happier to divorce Bill? I have my doubts.

Would it be good for her relationship with God? No. He wouldn't say, "Get out of there, Mary. My main concern is that you're happy, and you can't be happy married to that jerk." God would say, "My grace is sufficient for you, Mary. Lean on me, and I'll take care of you." The truth is, if Mary uses this trial as an opportunity to develop a close, intimate relationship with God, she could end up being thankful Bill didn't shape up right away! (Psalm 43:5, Matthew 11:28-30, 2 Corinthians 12:9, Romans 8:28, James 1:2-4)

Would it change Bill? That's hard to say. However, if he did change, Mary wouldn't benefit from it since she wouldn't be married to him anymore.

Option 2 *Keep trying to change Bill.* Would this make Mary happy? No. Bill has already shown that he's unwilling to change. Continuing to try to change him would only make Mary more angry and resentful. Would it be good for her relationship with God? I don't think so. Especially not if she harbored angry and hateful feelings toward Bill. Would it change Bill? It hasn't worked so far—probably not this time either.

Option 3 *Punish Bill. Do the work herself, but pay Bill back in other ways. Refuse to give him the things he wants from her in their marriage.* Would this make Mary happy? No. Revenge never makes anyone truly happy. Would it be good for her relationship with God? No, she would still be harboring resentment and anger. That wouldn't be good for her relationship with God. Would it change Bill? No. Instead, it would make Mary the bad guy, and Bill would feel like he had a right to not help with the housework since Mary wasn't meeting his needs either.

Option 4 *Do the work herself, but with a "poor me" attitude.* Would this make Mary happy? No. Would it be good for her relationship with God? No. Would it change Bill? No.

Option 5 *Escape. Do the work but reward herself with the leftover pie and ice cream once Bill and the kids go to bed.* Would this make Mary happy? Sure it would—for about ten minutes. But it wouldn't solve her problems, and she would be just as unhappy after she finished the pie and ice cream. Probably more so because she'd regret breaking her boundaries. Would it be good for her relationship with God? No, it would be much better for her relationship with God if Mary were to go to Him for deliverance rather than food. Would it change Bill? No.

Option 6 *Do the work herself and go to God for help in dealing with her attitude toward Bill.* There's no way that Mary could keep a pure heart toward Bill without God's help. To avoid angry, resentful feelings, she would need to continually renew her mind so she could see Bill and the situation through God's eyes. Would this make Mary happy? Yes. I think forgiving Bill is Mary's only real hope for happiness, but she would definitely have to go through a painful struggle and give up her own desires to get to that point.

Would it be good for her relationship with God? Yes, it would be great for her relationship with God. She would draw near to Him as she depended on Him in this situation, and she would become more like Him as she gave up the focus on herself and her rights. Would it change Bill? Maybe, maybe not, although I do think Bill would become more open to change if he were to see a godly attitude in Mary.

Option 7 *Forgive Bill and have the kids help her with the work.* Would this make Mary happy? Yes, and she would be less stressed out if she trained the kids to help. Would it be good for her relationship with God? Yes. Would it change Bill? Maybe, maybe not. However, if the kids were helping, life would be more manageable even if he didn't change.

Now this is all very interesting, but it looks time consuming, right? It actually isn't. I just wrote all that out to show you how I would evaluate each option. In practice, I just make a little chart. I put an up arrow if it will make me happy or close to God or change the situation and a down arrow if it does the opposite. If it's questionable, I make a question mark.

I'll let you fill in the chart below so you can see how easy it is to do. Use up arrows, down arrows, and question marks to fill in the columns. If you need help getting started, you'll find a completed chart on page 160.

	Happiness	God	Changing Bill
1. Divorce Bill.			
2. Nag at Bill - try to get him to change.			
3. Do the work but punish Bill in other ways.			
4. Do the work with a "poor me" attitude.			
5. Do the work and eat ice cream.			
6. Do the work cheerfully, submitting to the Lord and forgiving Bill.			
7. Forgive Bill and have the kids help with the work. Note: We'll learn how to forgive Bill in the chapter on anger!			

Now look back over the chart and answer the following questions:

Which options were best for Mary's relationship with God?

Which options were best for Mary's happiness?

_____

• Did you find anything interesting about the options that were best for making Mary happy?

_____

• Which options had down arrows all the way across? Did that surprise you? Why or why not?

_____

_____

I don't know about you, but in my natural unredeemed state, those middle options—the ones with all the down arrows—are just the sorts of options I tend to gravitate toward. I *think* those options will get me what I want. It's only when I use the truth to analyze the options that I see how bad they really are.

In order to have the strength to choose an option that involves submitting to God, I need to renew my mind and carry my thoughts captive to the truth. This is necessary because my thoughts left to their own devices are too busy crying out, "That's not fair!" to think about doing what God wants me to do.

I often use these charts to help me understand difficult situations, and I always come to the same conclusion—God's way is the best way even when it means dying to self. I have learned firsthand the truth of Matthew 6:33.

• How do you think Matthew 6:33 ties in with Mary's situation?

_____

_____

• What kinds of character changes could you see happening to Mary if she actively perseveres and submits to God in this situation rather than following her natural inclinations?

_____

_____

• What kinds of character changes could you see happening in her life if she follows her own inclinations and chooses to passively endure or escape?

_____

_____

Our actions *do* affect our character one way or another. If Mary continues to be angry with Bill, trying to change him so that she can be happy, she will very likely grow resentful and bitter. This could affect her whole personality and outlook on life.

On the other hand, if she works hard at forgiving Bill and accepting him as he is, she will likely become more accepting and less critical of other people as well. The way she responds in this situation will have an effect on her character and on her relationships with other people.

There is one other thing I'd like us to look at before we leave this example. Sometimes there is a practical solution to our problems. What practical solution was added to option #7?

_____

Can you think of any other practical solutions for Mary's dilemma?

_____

Mary's first concern is dealing with her own sin of condemning and possibly even hating Bill. She'll need to turn to God for help with that. Next, she should look at other possibilities to help with her problem of being overloaded. That might be having the kids help, hiring help, or adjusting her work schedule. It would also be good for Mary and Bill to see a counselor to help them come up with solutions to their problems. If Bill wasn't willing to go, Mary could go by herself.

Option Charts

Instead of journaling today, I'm going to ask you to try using an option chart to analyze a current trial. Use the chart on the next page and list your options like we did with Mary and Bill. Then tell how each option will affect your relationship with God and anything else you would like to get out of the situation, such as happiness, comfort, the easy life, or better relationships.

As you're doing this, remember not to waste energy thinking about options that don't exist (such as changing another person). If I'm doing this myself, I will actually write down what I *want* to be an option on the first line of my chart and then cross it out and write "NOT AN OPTION!!!!" next to it. This helps me drill it into my mind that I can't change reality.

Option charts are especially helpful in situations where you've truth journaled and the truth isn't pretty. Maybe you're in a situation you can't change (such as the death of a loved one), or maybe you're in a situation you can't change with a clear conscience (such as divorcing an annoying spouse).

With either situation, option charts will help you let go of the tendency to dwell on what life *should* be like and accept life in its "as is" condition. Personally, they always help me see that God's way really is best, which gives me the strength to do what He asks me to do.

Are you ready to try your own option chart? If you need help, see the chart on page 160 for an example. You can also see an example at barbraveling.com under the "Renewing of the Mind Tools" tab.

Think of a current trial and list your options in the column on the left. List two more things that you want up at the top next to "Relationship with God." Then evaluate each option by putting an up arrow, a down arrow, or a question mark in the box for that option.

	Relationship With God		

Before ending today's lesson, I want to say a word to anyone who is experiencing a trial because of abuse. When I speak of submitting to a trial, I'm not talking about abusive situations. If you or your kids are in this situation, please get help as soon as possible! Talk to your pastor, a counselor, a friend, or call an abuse hotline. If you're in a potentially abusive situation, don't wait until a line is crossed. Call a counselor today. They'll be able to help you walk through this.

DAY 4

Yesterday we talked about our options when it comes to trials. Although our natural inclination is to escape, obsess, or manipulate, we know that submitting to God is the higher road. The problem is doing it. Submitting to God when giving in and dying to self seems so unfair.

Today we'll look at a passage that will give us some ideas about how to submit. In Hebrews 12:1-15 the author talks about running the race that is set before us. The Greek word for race can also be translated as conflict or fight. Think of your trial as the "race" that you're running and then answer the questions on the following page.

Read Hebrews 12:1-15 and glance over the last five verses of Hebrews 11 to get the context for this passage. Name a few of the conflicts or trials that people were experiencing in Hebrews 11.

_____

Our trials are very different than those listed in Hebrews. You might say we have an easy life compared to them. The problem with the easy life is that we start to feel like we *deserve* the easy life. We deserve to have everything fair and perfect and easy.

This isn't true. God uses those unfair, hard things in our lives to transform us. As you study this passage, keep your own trial in mind. How can the words of this passage help you in dealing with *your* conflict?

Let's look more closely at Hebrews 12:1. What three pieces of advice does the writer of Hebrews give in this verse?

_____

_____

The strict interpretation of the Greek is "lay aside every weight and the easily besetting sin." Carrying around extra weight and sin hinders our walk with God and our ability to do what He calls us to do.

You and I both know the problems that come with extra weight. We get so used to carrying those extra pounds that we don't realize how much they're affecting our lives.

This always hits home to me when I go backpacking. I slip on a thirty pound pack and suddenly it becomes much more difficult to walk and breathe as I hike up a wilderness trail. I've learned to pack only necessary items so that I can reach my goal more easily.

It's the same in our walk through trials. Too much weight can keep us from reaching the goal of what God wants to accomplish in our lives. This weight can come in many forms: It may be bad habits. It may be unrealistic expectations. It may be lies that we believe. It may be too-busy lives. Or it may even be the weight of childhood experiences that we haven't worked through yet.

If we want to grow, we must lay aside those weights and cast off the sin that is so often attached to them. We'll practice doing that with another look at the life of Mary and Bill from yesterday's example.

In order to see how childhood experiences can be a weight, let's imagine Mary growing up in a child-centered family. Suppose her parents' main goal for her was to be happy. Imagine that Mary didn't have to contribute to household chores and was pretty much able to do whatever she wanted.

Can you think of any "weights" Mary might be carrying based on those childhood experiences?

_____

Can you think of any "easily-besetting" sin that might accompany the weight Mary brought from her childhood?

_____

_____

Mary might carry the weight of being accustomed to an easy life. She may have bad work habits if she was never trained to work. She may also believe the lie that she shouldn't have to do anything hard and may have the expectation that life should be easy.

Also, if she was used to her parents fixing all her problems, she may believe that she shouldn't have to deal with all these hassles with Bill. Since Mary also carries the baggage of our culture, which says it's okay to divorce over things like this, Mary might be tempted to divorce Bill as an easy solution to her problems.

Can you see how all these weights would affect Mary's ability to submit to God and accept Bill as he is?

It was perfectly appropriate for Mary to try to work out a more fair division of duties. But when Bill refused to change, Mary had a decision to make. She could either stand up for her "rights" and continue to be angry with Bill, or she could die to herself and live for God. Only one of those choices will draw her closer to God and develop maturity in her life.

If Mary chooses the narrow path and goes to God for help with this, she'll have to look at some tough questions: Does she *deserve* an easy life? Is it okay to ditch Bill just because he's selfish and lazy? Does she *really* need to lay down her life to love others well? Even when it's unfair?

It will be far easier for Mary to forgive Bill and accept him in his "as is" condition if she takes the time to carry her thoughts captive to the truth. Truth journaling, in this case, becomes a means of laying aside the weight so Mary doesn't become tangled up in her own sin.

Some other weights Mary may need to lay aside are conversations with people who tell her to stand up for her rights. They could be stumbling blocks if God is calling her to lay down her life. If her life is too busy, she may need to let things go so she isn't so stressed out. If she's a perfectionist, she may need to lower her standards. Examining her life will help Mary see what weights she needs to set aside.

I realize that what I'm saying is extremely difficult to do in practice. The culture is screaming at Mary not to let Bill get away with it. She deserves better! Mary will have to constantly compare what the world is shouting at her to what the Holy Spirit is whispering to her through God's Word.

And that's where that third piece of advice comes in. Mary needs to run her race with perseverance—there's that *hupomeno* word again. She needs to continually abide in the presence of God if she wants to shut out the voices of the world. It is only through the truth of God's Word that she can be set free from bitterness and anger in this situation.

What advice does the writer of Hebrews give us in Hebrews 12:2?

_____

This is good advice for two reasons. First, it will be a lot easier for Mary to submit out of love for Jesus than out of love for Bill. She's probably not feeling very loving toward Bill right now. Second, when Mary remembers what Jesus gave up for *her*, then what she's being asked to give up for Bill will seem small in comparison.

How does the message of Hebrews 12:7 help your attitude when you're going through a trial?

_____

Now think back to Mary's life again. If God wanted to discipline Mary in the area of her self-centeredness, do you think He'd be saying, "This is a horrible development in Mary's life; she needs to get out of that marriage so she can be happy"?

• What do you think God would say?

_____

_____

I think He might be saying, "Well, it's hard to see Mary in so much pain, and I'd certainly like to see a more Christ-like attitude in Bill, but I'm not going to take her out of this situation because I think it might help her overcome some of her selfishness if she can learn to submit in this."

Now if you've been in a situation like this, you might be saying, "But what about Bill? If Mary changes, then he gets off scot-free!" You know, Bill may be getting out of the work, but he's not getting off scot-free. One day he'll have to answer to God for his selfish attitude. Mary can't change him and she's compounding her suffering by being upset and angry about it.

If Mary submits to God and learns to see this situation from His perspective, she'll experience peace and joy in the midst of her suffering. He'll take away the angry feelings that are festering in her soul and making her so unhappy. Even if Bill doesn't change, Mary will be better off by submitting. In fact, God can bring great blessings into her life through this situation if she allows Him to use it for her discipline.

Read Hebrews 12:5-11 and record everything it says about discipline.

_____

_____

_____

Discipline is *not fun*, but it produces a harvest of righteousness and peace for those who have been trained by it. We don't always have control over whether or not we get disciplined, but we do have control over how we respond to it. Will we complain and feel sorry for ourselves, or will we allow the Holy Spirit to work in our lives?

Let's not focus on what we're giving up, but on what we're getting. The peaceful fruit of righteousness will be worth all that suffering.

Truth Journal

*Situation*_____

*Emotion*_____

*Belief*_____

_____

_____

*Truth*_____

_____

_____

_____

DAY 5

Today we're going to talk about failure because failure is a necessary part of success. We all know what it's like to get excited about a new weight loss program, do well on it for a while, and then experience defeat. Our thoughts immediately get negative: *This doesn't work! If only I could find a plan that works. Maybe I'll try something else.*

That's exactly what Satan wants us to think. He loves failure—the more the better—because he knows that the next step is self-condemnation. In fact, he's even willing to help us move along in that direction. Our failure is his opportunity.

We break our boundaries and Satan says, "You loser! You have no will power. Look at you! No wonder you're so fat!" God doesn't agree. He says, "Don't worry about it. There is no condemnation for those who are in Christ Jesus."

Satan says, "You'll never be able to lose weight and keep it off." But God says, "That's not true. You can do all things through Me. I'll strengthen you." Satan doesn't give up. He says, "If you're not skinny, you're nothing." God replies, "Man looks at the outward appearance, but the Lord looks at the heart." Satan keeps going: "You might as well give up. You know you can't do it." God doesn't agree. He says, "Don't become weary in doing good. At the proper time you'll reap a harvest if you persevere."

Do you see why it's so important to go to God for help the minute we break our boundaries? Replacing Satan's lies with God's truth is the only way we can make it through failure without giving up. If we do this, then failure becomes *God's* opportunity to work in our lives.

You may be doing really well right now. I hope so. However, please *mark this lesson with a paper clip* so you can come back to it if you go through a season of failure. Failure is a trial, but I'm afraid it's a trial most of us go through when we're trying to lose weight and keep it off. After all, if we could follow our boundaries perfectly right from the start, we wouldn't be having this struggle in the first place!

When you fail, try not to beat yourself up. Instead, go to God as soon as possible and truth journal or pray Scripture so you don't buy into Satan's lies. You could also renew your mind with the Bible passage we studied yesterday. I'll include Paul's advice to us below from Hebrews 12, along with some questions you can ask yourself when you've failed.

How to Handle Failure

1. Get rid of the weight.

Are you believing any lies that are making you want to eat? If you need help, look at the list of lies in Appendix A. Record any lies that you're believing and replace them with the truth.

Are there any other weights in your life that are making you want to eat? For example, do you have too much food in the house that you're tempted to binge on? Do you have unrealistic expectations for weight loss? Are you setting enough time aside each day to spend with God renewing your mind?

How about procrastination—is there something you need to get done that you're not doing? Do you have too much time on your hands? Are there any major emotions or situations fueling your desire to eat? If you can pinpoint why you feel like eating, it will be easier to come up with a plan of attack.

2. Get rid of the sin.

Are you involved in any sin that's making you want to eat? Are you holding onto resentment? Are you soaking in discontentment and forgetting to be thankful? Do you need to either forgive someone or ask someone to forgive you? Are you involved in something that you know is wrong? Go to God for help with your sin, and you'll lose the desire to go to food for help.

3. Run with endurance.

Remember the *hupomeno* word? If you're in the midst of failure, try to spend more time with God than normal. When I was in the early stages of breaking free from the control of food, I was surprised what a difference having a quiet time each morning made. Almost without fail, the days that I blew it were the days that I missed my time with God in the morning. My advice would be to have your regular quiet time in the morning and then renew your mind again at lunch and dinner. The more often you can renew your mind, the more likely you'll be able to get back on track quickly.

4. Fix your eyes on Jesus.

Remember how Jesus handled temptation? With Scripture! I've included some Bible verses at the end of this lesson that have been helpful to me when dealing with failure. Write them on index cards or an index card ring binder that you can slip into your purse if you're not at home. Read and pray through these several times a day if possible—morning, noon, and night. Your mind needs to be steeped in the truth in order to combat the lies of Satan.

5. Endure hardship as discipline.

Here's the great thing about failure: God can use it to build our character (Hebrews 12:11). Unfortunately, we don't always let the trial of failure train us. If you're like I used to be, then you're in the habit of giving up for a season so you can eat whatever you want. This is an escape mechanism. We eat to escape other trials in our lives. We also eat to escape the trial of trying to lose weight and failing at it.

Escape is the easy route, but it leads us away from God. He is the answer to failure. We need Him more than ever after we've failed because we're so vulnerable. He *wants* to help us, and He knows what we're going through (Hebrews 4:15-16). The sooner we turn to Him for help the better. Here are some Bible verses you can use to go to Him for help:

Bible Verses

Romans 8:1 Therefore, there is now no condemnation for those who are in Christ Jesus.

1 Samuel 16:7b Man looks at the outward appearance, but the Lord looks at the heart.

Philippians 3:13b-14 But one thing I do: Forgetting what is behind and straining toward what is ahead, I press on toward the goal to win the prize for which God has called me heavenward in Christ Jesus.

Romans 12:1-2a Therefore, I urge you, brothers, in view of God's mercy, to offer your bodies as living sacrifices, holy and pleasing to God; this is your spiritual act of worship. Do not conform any longer to the pattern of this world, but be transformed by the renewing of your mind.

1 Corinthians 6:12 Everything is permissible for me, but not everything is beneficial. Everything is permissible for me, but I will not be mastered by anything.

Hebrews 12:1b-2 Let us throw off everything that hinders and the sin that so easily entangles, and let us run with perseverance the race marked out for us. Let us fix our eyes on Jesus, the author and perfecter of our faith, who for the joy set before him endured the cross, scorning its shame, and sat down at the right hand of the throne of God.

Hebrews 4: 15-16 For we do not have a high priest who is unable to sympathize with our weaknesses, but we have one who has been tempted in every way, just as we are—yet was without sin. Let us then approach the throne of grace with confidence, so that we may receive mercy and find grace to help us in our time of need.

Philippians 4:13 I can do everything through Him who gives me strength.

1 John 4:4 You, dear children, are from God and have overcome them, because the one who is in you is greater than the one who is in the world.

Galatians 6:9 Let us not become weary in doing good, for at the proper time we will reap a harvest if we do not give up.

Never forget that it is truth—not self-control—that will set you free from emotional eating. Pray these Scriptures when you're feeling tempted. God's Word is powerful. As He fills your mind with truth of these verses, you'll see the stronghold of emotional eating begin to crumble

Why don't you give that a try now? Choose a few verses and write a Scripture prayer below.

_____

_____

_____

_____

_____

Truth Journal

*Situation*_____

*Emotion*_____

*Belief*_____

_____

_____

*Truth*_____

_____

_____

_____

Idolatry

We've all read the accounts of the Israelites worshipping the golden calf, and we've probably all thought the same thing: *Why would they think a statue of a cow could do anything for them? That's crazy.*

We think the Israelites were a little backwards, but are we really that different? Do we not have a tendency ourselves to worship and rely on things that are just as incapable of helping us? In fact, could it be possible that we've been making an idol of food? In this chapter we'll explore that idea together. We'll take a look at how idolatry hurts us and what we can do to get rid of the idols in our lives.

DAY 1

But they mingled with the nations and adopted their customs. They worshipped their idols, which became a snare to them. Psalm 106:35-36

We know that idolatry is the worship of other gods, but what exactly does that involve? Today we'll look at five characteristics of idolatry. As you come to them in the lesson, please write them on the lines below.

Characteristics of Idolatry

1._____

2._____

3._____

4._____

5._____

Let's begin by looking at the Ten Commandments in Exodus 20:2-6. What are the first and second commandments?

_____

_____

The second commandment expands on the first. God knew that if we were to make idols, we would have a tendency to put them before Him. Thus our first characteristic of idolatry is that it is anything in our lives that we put before God.

It didn't take Israel long to break the commandments. In fact, the Israelites have a long history of worshipping idols and then turning back to God. Let's learn a little more about their practice of idolatry in Isaiah 44:6-20. Read this passage and answer the questions below.

Read Isaiah 44:6-8. How does this passage tie in with the first commandment (Exodus 20:2-3)?

_____

The Israelites thought their idols would help them. We think that our idols will help us. What does this passage say about idols and the people who make them? (Isaiah 44:9-11)

_____

• Why do you think the Israelites felt the need to make idols when they had seen the mighty works of God and had experienced His provision for them? (See also Exodus 32:1.)

_____

In Isaiah 44:14-17, the man is tending to his trees. What three things does he use his tree for after he cuts it down?

_____

Isn't that interesting? First the man uses the tree to meet his legitimate needs—for warmth and a fire to cook his food. But with the remaining wood, he fashions an idol.

Don't we do the same thing? We take the good things that God has given us to meet our needs. Then we go a step beyond our needs and turn the thing (or person) that God has given us into an idol.

What two things does the man do with the idol he has created? (Isaiah 44:17)

_____

In the Old Testament, it's easy for us to see that they were worshipping an idol because it was so cut and dried. They created a figure and used it only as a god. It's a little more difficult for us to determine what we're worshipping as idols, but this last verse helps us with some clues. The man did two things with his idol. He worshipped it and he turned to it for deliverance. These are our next two characteristics of idolatry.

• Can you think of any ways in which you have worshipped food or turned to it for deliverance?

_____

How many times have I turned to food to ease my mental state? Although I don't talk to the food, my actions speak louder than words. "Deliver me from boredom! Deliver me from the stress in my life! Deliver me from this difficult relationship! Make me feel better!"

And eating does make me feel better—for about five minutes. Unfortunately, eating a bowl of ice cream doesn't change my life. The problems are still there when the ice cream is gone.

Food was given to us to nourish our bodies. I think God also planned it as a means of bringing people together in fellowship around the meal. But it was never intended as a source of deliverance for our emotional needs. God wants us to turn to Him when we're needy, not to food.

Before we move on to the remaining verses in this passage, I'd like to bring up the fourth characteristic of idolatry. The Israelites were known to make sacrifices to their false gods. Do we ever make sacrifices to food? I think so.

Look back to the first part of Isaiah 44:9 once more: *Those who fashion a graven image are all of them futile, and their precious things are of no profit* (NASB). Think of the word profit. In a business situation a profit is what's left over when you subtract the expenses from the revenues. Let's look at this for a moment.

• What are the good things (revenues) that emotional eating brings to your life?

_____

• What are the bad things (expenses or costs) that emotional eating brings to your life?

_____

_____

_____

Does the good really outweigh the bad? Is emotional eating worth it? Those bad things on your list are the *sacrifices* you've made to the idol of food. Like the Israelites, we've made sacrifices to our idol without gaining anything other than a good feeling. And even that soon disappears.

It seemed natural for the Israelites to sacrifice to their idols. They didn't see anything strange about it because their whole culture was busy doing the same thing.

It's the same for us with food. Most of the people we know eat for reasons other than hunger. It seems natural. We don't see the craziness of it because it's so common. We make sacrifices to our idol without even thinking.

Why couldn't the Israelites see the futility of worshipping their idols? (Isaiah 44:18-19)

_____

_____

This is hard to understand. Why would God close their eyes and hearts so that they couldn't see what they were doing? Read Psalm 81:8-13 for more insight. What is God's heart in this passage?

_____

God didn't give Israel over to their ignorance because He was being vengeful. He loved them. He wanted them to turn back to Him. Remember our study of trials in the last chapter? If we're determined to go our own way, God will let us. Yet His purpose is always that we might learn from our trespasses and come back to Him.

Let's go back to our passage in Isaiah 44. In verse 20, what turned the man aside in the first place?

_____

Do you see how this ties in with the first chapter in this Bible study? We began to eat for emotional reasons because we, like the Israelites, were deceived. We believed eating would make us feel better or help us in some way. Is it any surprise that God uses the truth to set us free, since it was deceit that started us down the wrong path in the first place?

Also look at the last sentence. Can the man save himself? No. Can we save ourselves? No. Goodness knows we've tried. But we can't do it on our own. This is the last characteristic of idolatry: *It is hard to give up.* Self-discipline isn't enough. We need God's help. Which brings us to the beautiful part of this passage.

What has God done for us and what does He want from us? (Isaiah 44:21-23)

_____

_____

Isn't that a great passage? God *loves* us. He wipes out our transgressions. He doesn't forget us. He redeems us. What could be better than that?

Truth Journal

*Situation*_____

*Emotion*_____

*Belief*_____

_____

_____

_____

*Truth*_____

_____

_____

_____

_____

DAY 2

Someone once said that the first step in overcoming a problem is to know that you have one. Likewise, the first step in overcoming idolatry is to recognize your idols. That can be difficult to do because often our idols are so subtle we don't even notice them. Here are some questions that will help you discover your idols. Answer them below or on a separate sheet of paper.

1. What do you feel like you have to have to be happy?

2. What do you do when you're depressed, hurt, angry, lonely, stressed, etc.?

3. What do you do to avoid doing the things you don't want to do?

4. What do you always make sure you have time for each day?

5. What could you not live without?

6. In what areas of your life, do you experience your greatest struggles?

7. What would you have a hard time giving up for a month?

8. Where do your feelings of self-worth come from?

9. What do you escape to when you're having a hard time in life?

10. When do you most feel like eating?

The last question may seem out of place, but it's there for a reason. Sometimes we turn to food because our other idols aren't meeting our needs. Food may not have been the original idol, but it becomes an idol when we consistently turn to it for deliverance.

For example, maybe my idol is an exciting life. I feel like I have to have some excitement in my life to be happy. If I'm at a boring stage of my life, then I might eat to try to provide the excitement that I crave. My original idol is excitement, but food becomes an idol when I turn to it to deliver me from boredom.

• Can you think of any examples of this in your own life?

_____

_____

Your answer to the last question on the list may also point out some problem areas in your life—areas you could work on if you wanted to improve your life. For example, if I eat whenever I'm dreading a task that I have to do, I may need to work on the problem of procrastination. Did you find any areas you could work on to improve your life?

_____

Here is a list of potential idols: Circle any that you might be inclined to elevate to that level.

possessions	*a clean house*	*a career*
comfort	*creativity*	*lack of conflict*
power	*people*	*a political regime*
ministry	*television*	*the Internet*
reading	*shopping*	*husband and kids*
alcohol	*an easy life*	*physical appearance*
success	*status*	*desire for approval*
relationships	*exercise*	*success of children*
a busy life	*church*	*accomplishments*
food	*fun*	*excitement*
control	*your to-do list*	*independence*

Back in the days of the Bible, they had to create their idols out of wood or metal or stone. In our modern society with all its luxuries, we have a huge variety of idols from which to choose.

If you look at the list, most of the items on it are good things. It's okay to want them. The problem comes when we feel like we have to have them or we begin to rely on them to cope with life. The more we cling to them, the more their grip on us tightens. Soon they control us.

Idols will never make us happy long-term. Only God can do that. Thankfully, He is able and willing to help us break free from our idols. We'll talk more about that in the next few lessons.

Truth Journal

*Situation*_____

*Emotion*_____

*Belief*_____

_____

_____

*Truth*_____

_____

_____

_____

DAY 3

God always has a reason for His commandments. He's not just trying to be mean and stifle us. He wants to be first in our lives because it's His rightful place, but He also wants to be first because He loves us and knows that idolatry is bad for us. We'll be looking at the harmful effects of idolatry in the next couple of days. As you come across each negative consequence of idolatry in your studies, please record it below. We'll look at the first four consequences today and the last three tomorrow.

Consequences of Idolatry

1. _____

2. _____

3. _____

4. _____

5. _____

6. _____

7. _____

Jonah isn't really a person you associate with idolatry, but that's where we're going to begin our study. He makes a remark about idolatry when he's inside the fish. Here's what he says in Jonah 2:8: *Those who cling to worthless idols turn away from God's love for them.*

If you're like me, you're thinking, "Why is Jonah talking about idolatry when he's inside the fish? I don't remember anything in that story about idolatry." Well, let's read Jonah and see if we can figure it out. Read the book of Jonah and answer the following questions.

What was Jonah's trial? (1:1-3)

_____

How did Jonah handle the trial? (1:3)

_____

This is classic—talk about a man saying no to God! Jonah doesn't mess around. He's doesn't want to do what God asks Him to do, so he runs away from God and jumps on a boat. This is unbelievable. How could you say no to the Living God when He asks you to do something?

We shake our heads in amazement at Jonah's gall, and then we turn around and do the exact same thing. We may not hear God's voice *out loud* like Jonah did. But we know He wants us to do something. And we say no. *It's too hard. We don't want to do that. We're too comfortable. We don't want to change.*

We're no different than Jonah.

We all know what happens next. Jonah runs away, jumps on a boat, gets tossed overboard by the sailors, and ends up being swallowed by a fish. A big fish.

The next scene is a great one. Jonah's sitting in the fish's stomach, and he's talking. Now if a man were to talk from inside a fish, wouldn't you be curious to know what he had to say? You can find his whole speech in Jonah 2:2-9. This is where Jonah gives his remark about idolatry that we talked about at the beginning of this lesson.

But how does Jonah's experience tie in with idolatry? Wasn't he just running from God? My friend, that's exactly what idolatry is: running from God. I once heard it defined as God avoidance.

We don't want to do what God tells us to do, so we escape. Just like Jonah. God wanted to give Jonah the strength to do what He asked him to do, but when Jonah disobeyed, He gave him a fish instead.

When we choose to go to an idol rather than to God, we miss out on God's love and faithfulness to equip us. We also miss out on the blessings of doing His will. And like Jonah, we often get disciplined. Nothing so drastic as being swallowed up by a fish, but discipline nonetheless. These are the first three consequences of idolatry. Don't forget to write them in on the space provided at the beginning of this lesson.

Jonah had a good reason for not wanting to warn the Ninevites. Nineveh was the capitol of Assyria, and the Assyrians were enemies of Israel. Jonah would have been happy to have God destroy them. He didn't want to be God's instrument of grace and mercy to those evil people.

If Jonah had taken the time to renew his mind and see the Ninevites like God saw them, He could have done what God asked him to do with a pure heart. But Jonah didn't take the time. Instead, he ran, and that is the fourth consequence of idolatry: It puts distance between God and us, and in the process, it hurts our relationship with Him. We run to our idols because we don't really want to do what God is asking us to do.

We do this without even knowing it. Someone hurts us, and all of a sudden we're craving chocolate. We don't stop to think, *Hmm, God wants me to forgive this person and turn to Him for comfort, but I don't want to—she doesn't deserve to be forgiven. I know. I'll just have a piece of that leftover chocolate cake and that will keep my mind off the problem.*

No, we don't stop to think. We just eat the chocolate and we immediately feel better. Just like Jonah felt better after running. Our idol has kept us from having to deal with our sin. God wants us to forgive, but it's so much easier and so much more fun to eat the chocolate.

• Let me ask you something—does God's way sometimes seem too hard? Explain.

_____

_____

The thing that God keeps teaching me over and over again as I write this study is that hard things are not necessarily bad things. Hard things make us grow. Hard things make us look more like God if we submit to Him. When we take the easy way out, we miss what He has to teach us through the situation. We come out of the trial looking the same way we did going into it and have nothing to show for all that suffering.

If only we could see that it's foolish to run from God. It's easy to see it in Jonah's life, but not in our own. We don't see that taking the easy way out may just be a way of running from God.

List some of the ways you run from God.

_____

_____

Jonah realized it was futile to run from God, and he repented in chapter two. What did Jonah recognize and what was he planning to do now? (Jonah 2:6-9)

_____

What happened next? (Jonah 2:10—3:10)

_____

So the people repented and God relented. This should be a "happily ever after" story, right? Wrong! What happens in chapter 4?

_____

How soon we forget. As we finish the book of Jonah, we find him in the midst of a major tantrum. He's not happy with the way God's running the show, and he's not afraid to tell Him so. Look at verse 9.

> God to Jonah: Do you have good reason to be angry about the plant?
> Jonah: I have good reason to be angry, even to death!

Doesn't that sound like a little kid? Do you think that's the way we sound to God?

> God to me: Do you have good reason to be angry about the things that person said to you?
> Me: I have good reason to be angry, even to eating a chocolate bar that's not on my boundaries!

We eat in response to our emotions, don't we? The purpose of lifetime boundaries is to keep us from doing that. Not just so we can lose weight, but also so we can learn to deal with our negative thoughts and emotions.

As we bring our thoughts captive to the truth, He will bless us in ways we can only begin to imagine. God is faithful. He accepts us as we are and moves us along to where He wants us to be. We just need to be willing to do what He asks of us.

Truth Journal

*Situation*_____

*Emotion*_____

*Belief*_____

_____

_____

*Truth*_____

_____

_____

_____

_____

DAY 4

Yesterday we saw how idolatry invites discipline into our lives and causes us to miss out on the blessings of doing God's will and His faithfulness to equip us to do His will. Today we'll look at three more consequences of idolatry. Don't forget to fill in your chart on yesterday's lesson when you come to them.

Let's begin by looking at the famous weight loss verse, 1 Corinthians 10:13: *No temptation has overtaken you but such as is common to man; and God is faithful, who will not allow you to be tempted beyond what you are able, but with the temptation will provide the way of escape also, so that you will be able to endure it.* (NASB)

This verse is helpful to us for obvious reasons, but there's another way to look at it that can also benefit us. You may remember that the Greek word for temptation can also be translated trial. (The word in this verse is the same one that's used in James 1:2.)

The phrase "way of escape" in 1 Corinthians 10:13 is from the Greek word *ekbasis* and can also be translated "result" or "outcome." It's a compound noun that means literally "out of walking" so you can see how they get two such different translations from it.

If we look at the verse with these two words, we would read, *"No trial has overtaken you but such as is common to man; and God is faithful, who will not allow you to be trialed beyond what you are able, but with the trial will provide the outcome (of the trial), so that you will be able to endure it."*

This gives the verse a whole new meaning. First of all, we know that the trial isn't too big for us. We *can* get through it without ice cream. And second, we know that we'll get something out of it to make it worth our while. Not a financial or material reward, but a change of character, a result of walking through the trial with the Lord.

What do we get out of walking through the trial with food?

———————————————————————————————

Maybe five pounds and a lack of character development? I guess when you think about it that way, I'd go for the walk *with* God and *without* the ice cream. The problem is that we don't think about it. We just do what feels good, and eating is what feels good.

Why does it feel so good? Because something about the act of eating neutralizes our feelings so that life doesn't seem so bad after all. That's our reward for giving in to temptation. It's a quick fix.

Now here is the interesting part. What does the next verse, 1 Corinthians 10:14, say?

———————————————————————————————

Isn't that interesting? God knows that trials make us want to turn to our idols for escape. He even warned us about it! He also knows that when we give into idolatry, we're missing out on the lessons He wants to teach us from the trial. That's the fifth consequence of idolatry: It keeps us from learning the lessons God wants to teach us, and our character suffers.

Now look at Hebrews 12:7. Why do we endure hardship?

_____

_____

Do we have to endure hardship in this day and age? Explain.

_____

_____

If I discipline my kids, they have to accept my discipline unless they run away. But as adults, we don't always have to accept discipline. And we have a lot more ways of escape available to us than the Israelites had. We don't need to waste our time building a golden calf.

We can watch TV, read a novel, go shopping, surf the Internet, or go out for lunch. You name it. We have a multitude of idols readily available to deliver us from the situations God wants to use in our lives to bring us to maturity.

• Can you think of any areas of your life where the idolatry of food has hurt your character development? Explain.

_____

_____

Idolatry keeps us from turning to God for help, but it does more than that. It also keeps us from recognizing the seriousness of our bad habits and sins, and it makes us comfortable with them.

Look at my problem with procrastination as a case in point. I didn't realize how bad it was until I stopped snacking. I just thought I was an unorganized, let's-have-fun sort of person. That was only part of the picture though. The rest of the picture was that I was also a let's-escape-to-my-idol-so-I-don't-have-to-face-reality sort of person.

My habit of eating to avoid work kept me so comfortable that I didn't mind my disorderly life. I couldn't see what a negative impact it was having on my energy, my attitude, my family, and my walk with God. Procrastination was keeping me from being all that God wanted me to be.

Adding boundaries to my life made me uncomfortable because it revealed so many of my problems. Thank God I couldn't think of another good escape. What I needed was the truth to set me free, not a new recreational pursuit to make me feel better.

My friend, don't expect growth to be fun or easy. It's usually uncomfortable, often painful, and almost always takes longer than you think it should take. You will often feel battered and bruised, and you'll be tempted to give up.

That's when you need to cling to the Lord. Failure is an inevitable part of growth. Learn from your mistakes and press on. And remember Paul's words in Galatians 6:9: *Let us not become weary in doing good, for at the proper time we will reap a harvest if we do not give up.*

Before we close, I'd like to briefly mention the last two consequences of idolatry. We've talked about how hard it is to give up our idols. One of the negative consequences of idolatry is that it can lead to addiction. It can also cause us to sacrifice things we don't want to sacrifice. We talked about that on page 57.

We only control our idols at the beginning. Soon, they begin to control us. We don't like what they're doing to us, but we don't have the strength to change our ways. Thankfully, we don't need to rely on our own strength. God is waiting to help. Why don't you spend some time with Him right now putting some truth into your system?

Truth Journal

*Situation*_____

*Emotion*_____

*Belief*_____

_____

_____

*Truth*_____

_____

_____

_____

DAY 5

Wouldn't it be nice if we could solve all of our eating problems in a day? Or even in a few months of consistent, each-day-better-than-the-last progress? Unfortunately, losing weight and keeping it off is not that easy.

Instead, it's more of a forward-two-steps-back-one-step process. I hope you're beginning to experience some success in learning how to deal with emotional eating, but if you're not, don't worry. You *will* change if you keep pursuing God and taking off the lies and putting on the truth. But that change won't come without a bit of failure.

You may even experience failure after you think you have the problem solved. That's what happened to me my first Christmas on the boundary system. Because I was no longer tempted to eat outside of my boundaries, I went all out making Christmas cookies with my kids. We made *six* kinds of cookies. I never would have done that in the past because of the huge temptation.

We put the cookies in the freezer to take out for dessert each day, and everything went well for about two weeks. Then the idea of having all those great cookies in the freezer got to me, and I decided to change my boundaries. *Two extra snacks a day won't hurt*, I thought. Of course you know what I ate for my snacks!

You can guess the rest of the story. One change in the boundaries led to a month without any boundaries. Food had become an idol in my life again, and I was worried. Did my plan not really work as I had hoped? Was I about to fall back into discouragement and failure?

Then I realized—it wasn't the *plan* that had set me free from the control of food. It was God, and He used the truth to do it. So I began to truth journal and pray through Bible verses whenever I felt like breaking my boundaries. Soon I was back on track and temptation was no longer my constant companion.

The answer to getting back on track wasn't resolve and determination. The answer was truth. I guess you could say I had to use resolve and determination to apply the truth to my life over and over again.

I had hoped for a quick solution to the weight loss problem. Instead, it was a long process of work and growth and failure and success. God, in His infinite wisdom, used the struggle to mature me in ways that I wouldn't have experienced in a quick-fix solution.

So please, *don't get discouraged if you fail*. Instead, analyze your eating for a couple of days. What's making you break your boundaries? Is there an area of your life you need to work on? Take those areas, one at a time, and begin working on them. As you do that, try to hold "skinny" with open hands.

Let me explain. The reason I wanted an immediate solution to my problem with emotional eating was that I wanted to be skinny. Every time I failed, I gained weight. It was discouraging having to lose those same pounds over and over again.

My obsession with being skinny was actually a deterrent to getting over the problem of emotional eating because I felt like I *had* to be skinny. So every time I would break my boundaries in a major way, I'd despair of ever losing weight and eat to console myself.

In order to break free from the control of food, I also had to break free from the need to be thin. The truth is, God never says we have to be skinny to be acceptable. It's the world that says we have to be skinny.

Our culture is obsessed with physical beauty, and it's easy to feel inadequate when we don't measure up physically. We'll have to be careful to look at ourselves through God's eyes, not the eyes of our culture. Let's look at what God says about beauty.

Read the following verses and jot their message down on the lines below.

1 Samuel 16:7_____

Proverbs 31:30_____

Galatians 1:10_____

Luke 16:15_____

1 Peter 3:3-4_____

- Can you think of some things that are highly valued in our culture that are detestable in the sight of God?

_____

_____

Do you think God detests the fact that so many girls are growing up thinking that their self-worth depends on how beautiful or how skinny they are? Do you think God detests the fact that kids are growing up thinking that as long as they're good-looking, athletic, and popular, that that's all that counts?

Often what is highly valued among men is detestable in God's sight. God created beauty. He gives athletic ability. Those are gifts. But He doesn't want our children to think that that's what is most important in life.

God looks at the heart. He cares about our character. Are we kind? Do we have self-control? Are we compassionate? Are we good? Those are the things God cares about. And they're the things we need to care about.

God must be very sad when He sees the emphasis we put on physical perfection. He created us, and He loves the way He created us. He didn't make us all one color, one size, and one shape. That would be boring.

When our culture says we have to look a certain way to be acceptable, it's an affront to the Almighty God who designed us just the way He wanted to design us. He thinks we're beautiful—*as we are.*

What does Psalm 139:13-16 have to say about this issue?

_____

_____

When we say, "I have to be beautiful," or "I have to be skinny to be happy," we're making an idol of looks. Isn't it strange that we can have an idol of looks and food at the same time? They certainly aren't complimentary idols, are they?

- Do you think that the idol of looks has a negative impact on our problem with food? Why or why not?

_____

_____

Probably the biggest way I see the idolatry of appearance hurting our efforts to lose weight is in the area of failure and perseverance. When we break our boundaries, we don't say, "Oh well, I'll just truth journal and press on." Instead, we say, "Well, I'm going to look fat anyway, so I might as well keep eating." For some reason, the reality of not having a perfect body makes us want to eat in despair. The world demands perfection, and we're not measuring up.

In order to change our behavior, we must change our focus. When we care more about what God thinks than what the world thinks, we won't feel driven to eat when we gain a few pounds. After all, God can teach us through our mistakes, and He doesn't demand physical perfection.

It's essential that we take the time to renew our minds when we break our boundaries and gain weight. If we don't, we'll be tempted to slip into self-condemnation and continue to eat without boundaries.

The following chart compares God's thoughts with the world's thoughts on this issue. I've listed the world's thoughts on the left side and left room for you to place God's thoughts on the right side. Please finish filling in the chart.

World	God
I need to wake up early enough to exercise and make myself look good.	You need to wake up early enough to spend time with Me so your insides look good.
I must look perfect.	
I need to be skinny to be beautiful.	
If only I were skinny, then I would be happy.	
Looks are everything.	

It's comforting to know that we are infinitely precious to God no matter what size we are. As you continue the study, try to focus on seeing yourself through His eyes. Not only will that make you feel loved and cherished, it will also help you lose weight!

Worry

Amy closed her book and turned out the light. As she pulled up the covers, her thoughts went to Daniel. Why wasn't he home yet? He usually called if he knew he was going to be late. She lay still, straining to hear the sound of his keys in the door, but all was silent. No Daniel. She tried to go back to sleep, but it was no use. Finally she gave up and headed for the kitchen. Maybe a bowl of cereal would help.

We can all relate, right? We tell ourselves there's nothing to worry about, but the voice inside our head replies, *Are you crazy? Something terrible has happened—you just don't know about it yet!* Too often we silence the voice by heading for the refrigerator.

This week we'll begin working on breaking free from the emotions that make us eat. We'll start with worry: why we worry, why we don't need to worry, and how we can stop worrying. We'll also look at a new tool we can use to handle our emotions in a healthy manner. It consists of three questions to ask ourselves when we're upset:

1. Do I need to change the way I think?
2. Do I need to act?
3. Do I need to submit to God?

As we go through the study this week, we'll use these questions to deal with the emotion of worry.

DAY 1

Sometimes worry slams us in the face, and we're almost paralyzed with fear. Other times it's just a thought hovering in the back of our minds, irritating, but hard to catch. We're not sure what's bothering us. We're just out-of-sorts.

If you have a general feeling of unease but you're not sure what's causing it, examine your thoughts to see if you're worried. Run through the events of the day in your mind.

Did you just say something to a friend that you shouldn't have said? Did a loved one just say something that made you worry about them? Are you afraid of failing in some area of your life?

After you pinpoint your fear, discuss it with the Lord. Paul tells us how to do that in Philippians 4:6-8. Before we look at that passage, let's take a look at the verses right before that passage. What does Paul tell us to do in Philippians 4:4-5?

_____

So instead of worrying, we're supposed to rejoice. At all times. That seems like a tough order, doesn't it? Hard to pull off if you're a worrier. Let's keep going. Verse five says, "Let your gentleness be evident to all." The Greek word for gentleness used here is *epieikees*.

This word is actually a compound word. *Epi* means "resting on or motion towards." *Eikees* means to give way or yield. So the word for gentleness could be further defined as "resting on or moving towards an attitude of giving way or yielding."

In other words, we're not supposed to be saying, "Life has to be *this* way." Instead, we should be working towards an attitude of being willing to accept whatever God allows. If you think of a gentle person, you don't picture her demanding her rights.

• Can you think of any reasons why it would be helpful to have this mindset when you think about your worries?

_____

Why do you think Paul added "the Lord is near" in verse five after telling us to rejoice and be willing to yield?

_____

If you knew beyond a shadow of a doubt that the Lord was near to both you and your loved ones, would it be easier to rejoice and be willing to yield when things weren't going well? Why or why not?

_____

_____

This is what we need to remember when we're worried: the Lord is near. Nothing happens unless He allows it to happen. We might not like what He allows, but we do need to accept it and trust Him. God knows everything, He can do anything, and He loves us. He's worthy of our trust.

The next verse, Philippians 4:6, has so much in it. First, are we supposed to be anxious about anything at all?

_____

Not big worries, not little worries, not monumental worries. We're not supposed to be anxious about *anything*. What are we supposed to do instead?

_____

Notice that we have a job. The verse doesn't say, "Don't worry about it. God will take care of it." Instead, Paul tells us to pray, supplicate, and thank. Now what does that mean exactly?

Supplication is prayer directed toward a specific request. So we're supposed to spend time in general conversation with God (prayer), in specific conversation with

Him about our concern (supplication), and we're supposed to mix it all together with thanksgiving.

I guess this begs the question, "What do we have to be thankful for?" Worry and thanksgiving don't really seem to go together, do they? The verse doesn't specify what we are to thank God for, but I have some ideas.

We can thank Him for how He has provided for us in the past. We can thank Him for how He is providing for us right now. We can thank Him for being trustworthy and for working everything out for good (Romans 8:28). We can thank Him for what He has already done in the lives of those we're worried about. And we can thank Him for who He is in the midst of our worrisome situations.

Praying with thanksgiving gets our minds off of our helplessness and onto God and His strength. He is able to handle our worries. He is the Creator of the universe after all.

As I wrote this chapter, I tried praying with thanksgiving for one of my own worries, and it really did change my attitude. It seemed a more thorough way to pray for the matter, and I felt myself at peace afterwards, which is exactly what is supposed to happen.

Look at Philippians 4:7. What two things will the peace of God guard?

Spending time with God in prayer and thanksgiving helps align our thoughts with His thoughts. When we think like He thinks—and not like the world thinks—our hearts will be at peace.

The Greek word for guard is the term used for a military guard. We could say that God's peace is guarding our hearts and minds just like a soldier guards the ones entrusted to his care.

• What kind of picture do you have in your mind of God's peace guarding your mind and heart when you think of a military guard?

Another passage that deals with fear and worry is 2 Chronicles 20:1-30. Judah was about to be attacked by Moab and Ammon, and the people were scared. They had ample reason to worry, but they chose another approach.

What did they do instead? (2 Chronicles 20:1-4, 12)

The Spirit of the Lord spoke through Jahaziel in 2 Chronicles 20:14-17. What words of instruction and reassurance did God give the people of Judah?

How did Jehoshaphat and the people of Judah respond to these words? (18-19)

_____

The next morning they left for the wilderness of Tekoa. Jehoshaphat's confidence in God's ability to deliver them was still unshaken. How do you know this? (20-22)

_____

Did you notice how closely this passage reflects the Philippians passage we just looked at? Jehoshaphat puts his requests before God (2 Chronicles 20:12), thanks Him before he has seen evidence of God answering his prayers (vs. 18-19), and experiences peace that passes understanding both before and after God delivered them (vs. 22, 30).

What this tells me about thankfulness is that 1) we need to give it *before* God answers, 2) we need to thank Him for what He has already done, and 3) we need to thank Him for what He is about to do.

It might not always turn out as well for us as it did for King Jehoshaphat. He got exactly what he wanted, but we know that life doesn't always work that way. Not everyone in the Bible got what they asked for and neither will we. Regardless, we thank God. It all boils down to faith. Can we trust Him? Is He trustworthy? The answer is a resounding yes.

DAY 2: What Others Think of Us

Yesterday we looked at some general biblical principles about worry. The rest of the week we'll be covering three different areas of worry: what others think of us, personal well-being, and concern for others.

With each area, we'll ask ourselves three questions: 1) Do I need to change the way I think? 2) Do I need to act? 3) Do I need to submit? At the end of each day, I'll also provide a journaling example of how you might journal these worries.

Today we'll look at the first class of worries: what do others think of us? We all want people to like us and respect us. When we sense that someone is unhappy with us, we begin to worry.

Do I need to change the way I think?

Picture this for a moment. You're in a deep relationship with a wonderful man who loves you like no man has ever loved you. He's tender, compassionate, accepting, and always has your best interest at heart. He's also rich, smart, powerful, and well respected. Basically, he's everything a woman could ever want in a man. And he loves *you*.

If you had this incredible, soul-satisfying relationship, would it really matter if the rest of your relationships left a little to be desired? If this amazing man thought you were wonderful, would it really matter what other people thought of you?

You may have guessed what relationship I'm talking about. That's right. It's our relationship with God. This unique relationship is available to all of us, but it comes at a price: We have to give up everything else to follow Him. That's the only way to develop an intimacy that satisfies. It's also the best way to stop worrying about what others think of us.

As women, we want other people to like us. In fact, we tend to think it's a terrible thing when someone doesn't like us, and we may stew about it for days. Would Jesus say that it's terrible if someone doesn't like us? Why or why not?

_____

What kind of attitude are we supposed to have towards others? (Phil 2:1-8, John 15:12-13)

_____

It's sad when others don't like us, but it's not terrible. Our duty is to love *them*, not get them to love us. If everyone in the world were to hate us (which is unlikely), it would still be okay because God would still love us.

• How would your life change if you were to focus more on loving others than on getting them to love you?

_____

People fail, but God doesn't. When we rest in His love, we don't need everyone else to love us. His love empowers us to reach out even to those who don't like us. There is freedom in letting go of the need to have everyone love us and treat us well.

Besides wanting everyone to like us, we also want them to think well of us. It bothers us when they don't approve of the things we're doing. Often we're more worried about what others think of us than we are about what God thinks of us.

• How does seeking the approval of others affect your relationship with God?

_____

_____

• How does trying to live up to the expectations of others get in the way of loving them with a 1 Corinthians 13 type of love?

_____

_____

When others don't approve of us, we have two temptations. One is to say, "Well, I can never please her anyway, so why bother?" The other is to say, "Oh no, she thinks I'm bad! What can I do to get her to like me or think well of me?"

What are the dangers of these two responses?

_____

_____

Both of these responses lead to immaturity because they're self-centered. The person with the first response may not change something in her life that God wants her to change, and the second person may change something that God doesn't want her to change.

We get in trouble when we live for man's approval because we can't always please God and others at the same time. Sometimes the people we're trying to please aren't living for God. Their ideas of how we should live our lives won't be the same as God's ideas. Other times, they may be living for God but just have different ideas of how to live life than we do, and God call us to live our own lives, not theirs.

What kind of response would God want us to have when others don't approve of us? (Galatians 1:10, Colossians 3:12-15)

_____

_____

It's good to look at what others have to say about us because there may be sin in our lives that we're not aware of. Don't give in to the tendency to say, "No one's going to tell *me* what to do!" Just because the other person is harsh in his criticism doesn't give us the excuse to continue sinning.

We must be willing to bend, change, and grow in any way that God might lead. It will be much easier to do this if we're living our lives to please God and not others.

Do I need to act?

Here are a few good questions to ask if you're afraid someone is mad at you or doesn't like you: Have you offended this person? Have you sinned against her? Have you caused discord by unnecessary behavior? Have you been selfish? If you can answer yes to any of these questions, then you may need to apologize, ask for forgiveness, make restitution, or work on changing your behavior.

Do I need to submit to God?

The sad but hard truth is that not everyone will like us or approve of us. Even harder, they may not be willing to forgive us when we sin against them. If we've done all that God wants us to do and the person still doesn't like us, then we need to give it up. Just say, "Lord, I submit to you. I'm willing to live in this situation even though it's hard, because I love you. I give it all up to you." And then let it go.

Journaling example

Here's an example of how you might truth journal a situation where you're worried about what others think of you.

Situation: Joan thinks her friend Amanda has been taking advantage of her. She spoke to Amanda about it, and Amanda got mad at her.

Beliefs: *1. Amanda is mad at me. 2. She thinks I'm selfish. 3. I shouldn't have brought it up. 4. She always has to have things her way. 5. I'm sick of always having to be the unselfish one in this relationship.*

Truth: *1. True 2. Probably true 3. There was nothing wrong with bringing it up. (Note: This is true as long as Joan brought it up in a loving manner with a non-condemning spirit.) 4. Amanda has a sin problem with selfishness. It's not surprising that this sin problem spills over and hurts me. She's like this with others, too. 5. I don't have to do everything Amanda wants me to do. It's okay if she's mad at me. I must live my life to please God, not Amanda.*

Joan will enjoy Amanda far more if she can learn to accept Amanda "as is" and stop worrying about what Amanda thinks of her. If she doesn't need Amanda's approval, she won't be angry with her when she doesn't get that approval. She also won't be as inclined to let Amanda take advantage of her. Joan also needs to look at her own character. Is she selfish? She must look to God for that answer, not Amanda.

In closing, read Psalm 118:5-9 and Psalm 27:1-8. Record the main message of each passage.

_____

_____

_____

_____

The best earthly relationship cannot top that of a truly intimate, life-giving relationship with God. And the more we go to Him for help with our earthly relationships, the closer to Him we'll be.

DAY 3: Personal Well-Being

Personal well-being. We can fit a lot of worries into this category, can't we? *Will I be able to get everything done that needs to be done? Will I be able to pay the bills? Will I recover from this disease or injury? Will I ever get a job? Will this relationship last?* These are all normal worries. Let's apply our three questions to this category of worries so we can learn to let go of them.

Do I need to change the way I think?

I love to go backpacking with my family. Once we hit the trail, life becomes very simple. No decisions to make other than where to set up camp. And no worries other than the weather.

And yes, the weather actually *can* be a worry. It's a different experience to be totally dependent on God to keep you safe. During a scary thunderstorm, high in the mountains with only the thin fabric of your tent for protection, you realize that you are completely at the mercy of God.

You know, it's like that in regular life. We are *always* completely at the mercy of God. We just don't realize it because we have houses and food and jobs. We're used to being able to take care of ourselves without God's help.

When we find ourselves in a situation we can't fix, we worry because we think we need to do something, but we can't think of anything to do. We're so used to being in control that it's a scary and often foreign feeling to realize that we're *not* in control.

It helps to remember that nothing happens without God both knowing about it *and* allowing it. If He allows it, then we don't need to worry about it. He can do anything, including bringing wonderful things out of our worrisome situations (Romans 8:28).

The bottom line is, "Do we trust God?" We will never understand all that goes on in our lives and in the world, but we don't need to. God is in charge, and we must trust Him even when life seems harsh.

• Psalm 18:1-3 lists many reasons why we can turn to God and trust in Him. What are they?

_____

_____

_____

• God is all of these things, yet we still have a tendency to turn to food rather than to God when we're worried. Is food really a good refuge, though? If you were to write a Psalm-like paragraph about food and its trustworthiness, what would you write? Remember to look at the whole truth.

_____

_____

_____

_____

We often turn to food as a refuge because life isn't measuring up to our expectations. Because our culture puts so much emphasis on living the good life, we tend to worry when things go wrong. How can we be happy if we have to suffer? We feel like we need to be living our dreams in order to be happy.

Unfortunately, we forget about God in the dream. Even as Christians, it becomes more about living a great life rather than loving a great God. Jesus knew that we would have these tendencies. He talked about it in Matthew 6:25-34. Before we read this passage, lets look at Matthew 6:19-24 to get the context. What is the message of those verses?

_____

Now read verses Matthew 6:25-34. What *can't* we change by worrying?

_____

If you think about it, can you change anything by worrying? Not really, right? You can sometimes change things by acting or praying or even by submitting, but you can't change things by worrying. It's a worthless pursuit.

• If you really practiced the admonition in Matthew 6:33, how would your life change?

_____

_____

I've experienced the reality of this verse over and over again. The more I put God first in my life, the more He adds to it. I can't begin to describe the incredible richness He has brought into my life through His love and care.

Yet putting Him first hasn't been easy. I've had to do things I didn't want to do, accept things I didn't want to accept, and stop trying to change people I wanted to change—and that was just for starters!

Each time I submitted to God, I *thought* I was giving up the good life. I was willing to do what He wanted me to do, but I knew that life was going to be miserable.

I was wrong. More than wrong. Each time I sacrificed and put God first, I found joy. Sure, the joy was mixed with tears now and then as I died to self, but God was always there to lift me up.

Seeking God first is a journey. It doesn't happen in a day, but it can begin in a moment. As we die to ourselves, day-by-day and situation-by-situation, He will meet our needs "and all these things shall be added unto us."

Do I need to act?

Worry is a good emotion for taking action. Often we worry when what we should be doing is acting. No, we can't fix everything, but there are usually things we can do to help our situations.

For example, if we're worried about finances, we could see a financial counselor, go on a budget, cut down on our expenses, or move to a less expensive city. If we're worried about our marriages, we could talk about it with our spouses, go to a counselor, or work on our own faults in the marriage.

There are usually things we can do to help our circumstances, but often we are so overwhelmed with the magnitude of the problem that it seems too big to work on.

• Can you see any value in taking little steps to help a situation? If so, what?

_____

Is there anything in your life that is so overwhelming that you've been trying not to even think about it? If so, list two small steps you could take to help that situation.

_____

_____

If you think about it, very few problems are solved in an instant. We learn perseverance as we continue working towards a goal when it's difficult to do so.

Another thing that stops us from working on problems is the idea that things have to be done a certain way. I might say, "Well, there's no use working on my finances or marriage unless my husband's willing to work on it, too." This kind of attitude would make me not want to do anything unless my husband was doing it also.

Certainly, it would be easier in this situation if both husband and wife were on board. But that's not always real life. Sometimes one person wants to change and the other one doesn't. That's okay. We can't always have life the way we want it.

Pray about it and ask for God's help. There may be some things you can do to help your situation. You can't change other people, but you can change yourself through the help of the Holy Spirit.

Is there a worry in your life you haven't been dealing with because you're waiting for someone else to "get with the program"? What small step could you take now to improve the situation that you're worried about?

_____

Do I need to submit?

Have you been saying, "I can't be happy without _____ in my life"? The only good answer to that question is God. If I'm filling in the blank with anything else, then there's a good chance I'm making an idol of whatever it is I'm filling in the blank with.

To fully submit to God in the area of personal wellbeing is to say, "Even if this terrible thing happens to me, I will be okay because the Lord is with me. I give up my need to have life safe and comfortable and enjoyable." Only then can we become truly free of worry in this area.

Journaling example

Situation: Nancy is worried about losing her job.

Beliefs: *1. I'm going to lose my job. 2. How will we ever pay the bills if I lose my job? 3. We'll end up losing the house. 4. The kids will be devastated.*

Truths: *1. This is possible. 2. I could make money in other ways. I might be able to find another job. If not, I could take in some kids to babysit. There is also unemployment as an option. I might not be able to make as much as I do now, but I can still make enough to help with the bills. 3. I think we'll be able to cover the house payment if we cut down on our other expenses. If we do end up losing the house, God will have allowed it to happen. We could also put it up for sale and buy a smaller house. 4. Cutting down on our lifestyle will definitely affect the kids, but it may not be all bad. It could even end up being good for their character. I can be an example to them as I show by the way I live my life that God is more important than money.*

In order to break free from her worry, Nancy will need to stop thinking about what she can't change and concentrate on the things she *can* change, such as cutting down on expenses and looking at other options for income. She also needs to be willing to accept financial disaster if that's what God allows.

DAY 4: Concern for Others

I'm not sure if there is anything more painful than watching our loved ones suffer. We want to wrap our arms around them and make their problems go away, yet we're often powerless to help them. What can we do? We can't cure their cancer. We can't heal their relationships. We can't solve their problems. Instead, we often have to just sit there and watch them suffer. It's hard not to give in to worry.

Do I need to change the way I think?

There are three things we'll need to remember if we want to stop worrying about our loved ones: 1) God knows everything and we don't, 2) God can do anything and we can't, and 3) God's in control and we aren't.

Faith is the answer to worry. If God can do anything, then He can take care of our loved ones. If He chooses to allow suffering into their lives (and ours), then we need to accept it and trust Him.

Proverbs 3:5-6 says, *Trust in the Lord with all your heart and lean not on your own understanding; in all your ways acknowledge Him, and He will make our paths straight.* Can you think of any ways that leaning on your own understanding makes you worry about your loved ones?

_____

_____

• Why might God allow suffering in the lives of your loved ones?

_____

I sometimes wonder how Jesus felt about leaving His disciples and other loved ones when He ascended into heaven. Did He suffer, knowing that He'd no longer be in their presence as a man? Was it hard for Him to let go and let the Father take care of them? Was He tempted to worry about them?

In John 17 we see the prayer Jesus prayed for His followers before He left. He was obviously very concerned about how they'd do when He was no longer physically with them. By looking at how Jesus prayed for His loved ones, we can see how we are to pray for our own loved ones.

Read John 17 and list the things Jesus prays for regarding the ones entrusted to His care.

_____

_____

_____

_____

• When Jesus prayed this prayer, He knew His loved ones would have to suffer for their faith (John 16:31-33). Was His main concern for their happiness? If not, what was He concerned about?

_____

_____

God has a reason for allowing us to suffer. He also has a reason for allowing our loved ones to suffer. If they're not Christians, He wants them to believe. If they are Christians, He wants them to grow. Often we just want them to be happy. We'll feel better when we see life from God's perspective because it will remind us that He can use hard things for good in their lives, and that it's not the end of the world if they go through a little unhappiness along the way to spiritual maturity and a deeper walk with Him.

• How would keeping God's priorities in mind change the way you respond when your loved ones go through difficult situations?

_____

_____

The most important thing we can do for our loved ones is to pray for them. If we have children in the home, we need to seek God's wisdom in how to pray for them and how to talk to them about the trials they're going through. If life is all about fun and comfort, then trials are all bad. If life is about loving God and others, then trials are to be expected. Love involves sacrifice.

Think of a trial your loved one is going through right now. Can you see anything God could do in his or her life through this trial?

_____

How does God want you to view this trial? How does He want you to pray for your loved one?

_____

_____

Do I need to act?

Sometimes our loved ones have problems that can't be solved unless God intervenes, such as a terminal illness. Other times, they have problems that *can* be solved, but they don't want our help in solving them! And sometimes they have problems we can help with, and they welcome our help.

If you're struggling with how to help a loved one who needs help but doesn't want it, pray for guidance and seek advice from wise friends or professionals. This may be one of those situations you just have to accept, but it would be helpful to get some other opinions.

If you're worried about your children who are living at home, you have a little more control because you get to set the rules. If you have Internet access, put safety controls on it so you don't have to worry about it. Check out their computer games. Do they have a television or computer in their bedroom? They don't have to do things just because their friends do them.

It is *okay* to make rules that your kids won't like if it's for their welfare. Expect them to be upset with you every once in awhile! The more we seek to please God rather than our kids, the better we can love our kids.

Parenting in today's culture is so difficult because of all the temptations our kids face. If you're struggling with how to parent, seek counsel from God's Word, ask wise friends for advice, read great parenting books, seek out professional help, and above all, pray, pray, pray!

Are you worried about any loved ones right now? If so, who are you worried about and why are you worried? Are there any actions God wants you to take to help them? Are there any actions He wants you to *stop* taking?

_____

_____

One last thing to remember in this area is that "happy" shouldn't be our main goal for our kids. Just like us, their purpose in life is to love God and others. If we focus all our efforts on making them happy, we're helping to create demanding kids who are focused on themselves and not on God and others.

Do I need to submit?

Do you need to give this loved one up to the Lord? Are you hanging onto him too tightly? Are you saying, "He *has* to put God first in life," or "It's terrible if he's unhappy," or "She *has* to be healed?" It's easy to make idols of our loved ones. The more we hold them with open hands, willing to let anything happen, the less we'll worry.

It also makes logical sense to hold them with open hands since we can't control them anyway. In many situations our only choice is to accept what's happening with a *good* attitude or a *bad* attitude because there is nothing we can do about it. The sooner we accept it, the better.

It helps to remember that God knows everything about the situations that worry us, that He has far more resources at His disposal than we do, and that He loves our loved ones more than we do.

Is there anyone you need to hold with open hands? Explain.

Journaling Example

Situation: It's 11:30 p.m. and Amy's teenage son Daniel is 30 minutes past his curfew. She tried calling him, but he didn't answer. Amy is planning to wait 15 minutes before calling his friends and their parents. While she waits, she decides to truth journal.

Beliefs: *1. I can't believe Daniel isn't home yet. 2. I never should have let him go. 3. Where is he??? 4. He probably got in a car accident and is lying dead alongside the road somewhere. 5. If only I hadn't let him go.*

Truth: *1. This is not completely shocking. He usually calls when he's late, but not always. 2. That's not true. It was a good decision. I can't keep him home all the time just because something might happen when he's driving. 3. I don't know, but God knows and He loves Daniel even more than I do. 3. If that happens, it will be so unusual that it will make the news. Most kids who are home late don't make the news. They just make their moms worry. It will be very surprising if he's dead. 5. God allowed me to let him go so I don't need to worry about it. Whatever happens, happens. Lord, I love you, I trust you, and I worship you. May your will be done in my life and Daniel's.*

When I'm in a situation like this, it always helps me to pray with thanksgiving. The more I dwell on who God is in the midst of the situation, the less I worry because I know I can trust Him. I also have to accept the fact that my worry might come true. If I'm not willing to accept that possibility, I won't be able to let go of my worry.

• In closing, read Isaiah 26:3-4. Who will God keep in perfect peace?

_____

Why do you think it's so hard to trust God?

_____

If you struggle with worry, don't forget to try praying with thanksgiving. The more we make life about God, the less we'll worry. And one of the best ways to make life about God is to develop a thankful spirit. Not just thankful for the things He gives us, but thankful for who He is in the midst of the things He *doesn't* give us.

DAY 5

Today I'd like to take a break from our regular Bible study and check in with you to see how you're doing with eating. Answer the following questions with your weight loss struggles in mind.

What emotions or situations cause you to eat the most?

_____

_____

• What would you say is your biggest problem right now when it comes to eating?

_____

• What lies are you believing that contribute most to eating outside of the boundaries or eating too much at meals? (See Appendix A if you need help.)

_____

_____

_____

List the truth for each of those lies.

_____

_____

_____

_____

It's easy to get caught up in trying to follow the boundaries and forget that it's the truth that sets us free, not the boundaries. We'll only be able to follow our boundaries if we have iron willpower or if we apply the truth often enough that we actually *want* to follow our boundaries.

We've discussed several different ways to put the truth into our lives: Bible study, Scripture prayers, Bible verse memorization, truth journaling, option charts, and the questions, "Do I need to change the way I think? Do I need to act? Do I need to submit?"

What have you been doing to put the truth into your life on a regular basis?

_____

How much time have you been spending each day applying the truth to your life?

_____

How much you change and how quickly you change will both be determined in large part by how much time you spend getting rid of the lies you believe and replacing those lies with truth.

Listen to John 8:31-32: *So Jesus was saying to those Jews who had believed Him, "If you continue in My word, then you are truly disciples of Mine; and you will know the truth, and the truth will make you free."*

The literal Greek translation is "abide in My word." The word abide has a sense of permanence about it. This isn't just a quick little visit to the Word now and then. Instead we are called to *live* in the Word. To think about it throughout the day and use it to guide our lives.

According to the verses you just read, what will happen if you abide in God's Word?

_____

_____

Do you think you can break free from the control of food just by dabbling in the truth every once in awhile? Why or why not?

_____

_____

John 15:1-6 also speaks of abiding in Him. What can you learn about abiding from these verses?

_____

_____

If I cut a branch off my apple tree, it not only won't bear fruit, but any fruit that was there when I cut it off will also die. It would be ridiculous for me to leave that branch on the ground and expect it to have apples next year.

My friend, it's just as crazy for us to expect to bear fruit in our own lives if we're not abiding in God's Word. We must abide in Him and in His Word so His power can flow into us and His truth can set us free.

If you're already abiding in His Word, yet struggling with a particular sin or bad habit, then you need to apply His truth directly to that area of your life. Find some Scriptures to pray through that address your problem, ask a friend for help with prayer and accountability, and spend the time you need to renew your mind in that area.

When I began to work through my own problem with emotional eating, I was already abiding with the Father and in His Word. Since I was still struggling, I knew there were probably some lies at work in my life that were making me want to overeat.

I decided to try truth journaling *every* time I broke my boundaries, even if it was just by one bite. After several weeks, I began to notice a difference in the way my mind was working.

First a normal thought would come into my head: *Those cookies were so good. I should have a few more.* Then a new thought would pop up: *You'll never have enough cookies to satisfy you; it's better to stop at just one or two.*

Or I'd think, *I deserve a treat after all that hard work*, and the new thought would say, *A treat isn't a reward. It's a punishment.*

The Holy Spirit was working in my life through the truth, and it was becoming easier to follow my boundaries. The other thing God used (and is still using) to help me break free of this stronghold is Scripture prayer.

I often pray through the verses on page 53 when I'm struggling, and I'm always amazed at the power God releases into my life through His Word. After only a few days of praying through those Scriptures, I'll find my desires lining up with His desires again. His truth really does set us free. We just need to take the time to abide in it.

Is there anything you need to change in order to help you gain victory over emotional eating?

_____

_____

_____

Discontentment and Boredom

Michelle picked up a magazine and idly flipped through the pages. Finally, she thought, they're all quiet. It had been a normal morning. Spilled cereal at breakfast, the usual squabbles about toys, mountains of laundry, and finally the long awaited nap. At least long awaited by her. They hadn't exactly been clamoring for it. She loved the kids of course and was glad she could stay home with them, but sometimes the monotony got to her. Especially in the winter. I know, she thought, I'll eat that leftover cake. Maybe that will perk me up. Michelle tossed the magazine aside and headed for the kitchen.

If you pick up any women's magazine these days you'll find articles on improving your life. Their headlines fuel our imagination: *Live your dream! Find your passion! You can have it all!*

The problem is that we *don't* have it all. No one's life is perfect, and we all suffer from different forms of hardship. Yet because our culture tells us that we need a wonderful, fulfilling life—that we *deserve* it, in fact—we begin to feel discontent when life doesn't measure up to our expectations. This week we'll be focusing on the answer to the problems of discontentment and boredom.

DAY 1

You've heard the phrase. *Well, as long as he's happy, that's all that matters.* It sounds noble. Happiness is more important than money. Happiness is more important than a prestigious job. Happiness is more important than living the materialistic lifestyle. But is it a noble phrase? More importantly, is it a *true* phrase? Would Jesus have said, "Well, as long as you're happy, that's all that matters"?

What do you think He would have said?

_____

_____

It's an eye-opening question, isn't it? You know what I think He would have said? "Well, as long as you love me and put me first in your life, then it doesn't really matter if you're happy, because I'm going to give you joy. Living for yourself will never make you happy."

That's a radical thought. Even as Christians, we tend to think we need a certain lifestyle or relationship to be happy. So when we're unhappy, we don't go to God to see life from His perspective. Instead, we get lost in if-only land: *If only I were married. If only I had a better relationship with my husband. If only I had a better job. If only I had more friends. If only I had children. If only the kids would get along.*

Let me ask you a question. Try to be honest. What do you feel like you need to change in your life to be happy?

_____

We often think we can't be happy unless our lives change in some radical way. But is that true? In other words, if we had the means to make our lives exactly the way we wanted them to look, would we be content? Think about it. If that's not true, then we can give up the idea rolling around inside our heads that says, "Life has to be *this* way in order for me to be happy."

Let's look at a man in the Bible who had the means to make himself happy. King Solomon had all that money and power could give him. He had beautiful houses, beautiful gardens, good food and entertainment, lots of money, and three hundred concubines.

Now, the great thing about King Solomon is that he was a wise, analytical person. He didn't just enjoy his lifestyle—he analyzed it for us and then recorded it for history. The book of Ecclesiastes is a record of his search for happiness. As Solomon tried different things in life to make himself happy, he began to cast them out one by one, saying, "This is meaningless; this is folly." What were some of the things he rejected as folly?

Eccl. 1:16-18 _____

Eccl. 2:1-2 _____

Eccl. 2:4-11 _____

_____

Eccl. 2:17-19 _____

Eccl. 4:4 _____

Well that pretty much covers it, doesn't it? If a person could be fulfilled by what life had to offer, King Solomon should have been able to make it happen. But he couldn't.

What was his conclusion at the end of the book? (Eccl. 12:8)

_____

Ecclesiastes 5:10 gives a clue as to why Solomon found life to be meaningless. It also shows us why we won't find lasting happiness by searching for it in a great lifestyle. How does this verse apply to our search for fulfillment?

_____

_____

Basically, what Solomon is saying is this: *Don't waste your time trying to be filled with what the world has to offer. You'll never get enough to satisfy you.*

In other words, if you're trying to find happiness in food, you'll never have enough food to satisfy you. If you're trying to find happiness in a relationship, it will never be good enough to satisfy you. If you're trying to find happiness in your accomplishments, you'll never get enough done in a day to satisfy you.

My friend, if we're trying to fill ourselves up with anything other than God, we will *never* be satisfied. God created us to worship Him alone, and He won't allow us to be happy with anything else.

In the end, what did all of Solomon's riches and the lifestyle that went with it do for him? (1 Kings 11:4-6)

_____

• People who travel to poor countries often comment on how happy the people are there. Do you think contentment is more a problem of the rich than the poor? Why or why not? Why do you think so many are discontent in rich countries?

_____

_____

Jeremiah 2:11-13 talks about the tendency we have to try to fill ourselves with the creation rather than the Creator. What two sins did the people commit in these verses?

_____

_____

We all have a tendency to dig our own cisterns, trying to fill ourselves up with the things of the world rather than with God. Think of your own life. What do you try to fill yourself up with?

_____

What do the Israelites' problems seem to stem from? (Jeremiah 2:14-24)

_____

What were the Israelites saying in Jeremiah 2:25?

_____

Do you see how closely discontentment ties in with idolatry? When we try to solve our discontentment apart from God, it leads to "digging our own cisterns." Those cisterns become idols that we put before God.

When we try to meet our needs with the gods of our culture, we will never have lasting contentment. Our moods will be dependent on our circumstances. Discontentment is an opportunity for us to look at our beliefs. Are we living for God and believing what He says in the Bible? Or are we being taken in by the world and believing what it has to say? Let's compare the two for a moment.

What does the world say you need to be happy?

_____

• What does God say that you need to be happy?_____

• In fact, does God even say that you need to be happy?_____

In a way it's comforting to know that we can't create lasting happiness just by shaping up our lives. It's comforting because we can't always create the lives we think we need to have to be content. Only God can give us lasting contentment. That's a blessing because God is always there.

Let's close by looking at Ecclesiastes 12:13-14. What are Solomon's final words of advice after searching the world for happiness?

_____

DAY 2

Do you ever try to set up your life just right so you can be comfortable and happy? And then, just when you think you have it all together, something happens to mess it all up? I think we've all had that happen to us. Thankfully, we don't need perfect lives to be happy. Let's see what John has to say about this in 1 John 2:15-17:

Do not love the world nor the things in the world. If anyone loves the world, the love of the Father is not in him. For all that is in the world, the lust of the flesh and the lust of the eyes and the boastful pride of life, is not from the Father, but is from the world. The world is passing away, and also its lusts; but the one who does the will of God lives forever. (NASB)

Although there is nothing wrong with trying to improve our lives, it becomes a problem if we put all of our efforts into creating a great life and make that more important than loving God and others. If you think of all the great believers in the Bible, many of them had less than ideal lifestyles.

In 1 John 2:15-17, John tells us not to love the things in this world. He then goes on to divide the things of the world into three categories. What are they?

_____

Do these three things ring a bell? If you think back to the temptations of Jesus, these were the exact three things that He was tempted with. Turn back to Luke 4:1-13 once again. What was the first temptation?

_____

This corresponds to the lust of the flesh—our fleshly desires. For Jesus in this passage, it was food. After all, He had just gone forty days without eating. Food would definitely be appealing.

What are some fleshly desires we might be tempted with?

_____

What was Jesus's second temptation? (Luke 4:5-7)

_____

Do you see how this temptation corresponds to the lust of the eyes? Jesus had everything before him man could ever want, and He turned it down. What Scripture did He quote as He turned it down? (Luke 4:8)

_____

Why do you think He quoted that Scripture?

_____

List some temptations we might face in the "lust of the eyes" area.

_____

I think there's more to this temptation than meets the eye. Often we want what we see others having. Material possessions automatically come to mind, but there's more to it than that. This temptation can also apply to relationships.

For example, are you satisfied with being single if you're single? Are you satisfied with being married if you're married? Are you satisfied with your *husband* if you're married?

Sometimes our expectations in relationships are so high that no one can live up to them. We see other great relationships out there (often in movies and novels) and we think, "Why can't I have a relationship like that?" The lust of the eyes has made us demanding and ungrateful.

• Think about your own life. How do you think God wants you to view life if you're not in a relationship? How do you think He wants you to view your husband if you're married?

_____

• How do you think Satan wants you to view life if you're not married? How do you think he wants you to view your husband if you're married?

_____

_____

• Do you think romantic movies and romance novels promote Satan's agenda when it comes to causing dissatisfaction in both the single life and marriage? Why or why not?

_____

_____

We need to remember that novels and movies are make-believe. It's easy to have a perfect relationship if you're reading through a script with a man who is paid millions of dollars to have a perfect relationship with you. It's not so easy in real life. In real life, we're sinners who hurt each other on a regular basis.

Not only are we sinners, but we are also inherently different than our husbands and boyfriends. Just look at little boys and girls play or drive a bunch of teenagers around town. You'll hear very different conversations coming from the boys than you will from the girls.

Expecting our men to be perfect on a conversational and emotional level is just as unloving and ungracious as men expecting women to be perfect on a physical level.

Yes, we can work on better relationships, but we need to do that within the context of love, grace, and realistic expectations. We do that best if we do it from a position of relying on God to get our emotional needs met. Because when He is meeting all of our needs, it's much easier to give grace to the people in our lives who aren't meeting them.

Let's go back to our passage in Luke. What was the third temptation Jesus was faced with? (Luke 4:9-10)

_____

In this temptation, Satan appeals to Jesus's pride in a couple of different ways. First he says, "*If* you're the Son of God," and second He gives Jesus this glorious picture of Jesus falling off the roof with all the angels taking care of Him. That would prove to everyone that He really was who He said He was—the Son of God.

We have the same temptation. We want to show people that we really *are* worthwhile, that we're not as bad as they think we are. We do different things to show them: We brag. We accomplish. We pretend. We people please. We try to impress. And we may even try to lose weight.

It's so easy to get caught up in seeking the approval of man rather than God. This hurts our relationship with God, and it also contributes to our discontent. We're much happier when we're only seeking to please God.

• Think of your own life. What happens when you constantly try to live up to the expectations of others or try to get them to like you and think well of you?

_____

_____

_____

How would your life change if you were to care more about what God thinks and less about what others think?

_____

_____

_____

I find it fascinating that the three things John warns against in 1 John 2:15-17 are the same temptations Jesus faced in the desert. Is it any surprise that we struggle with the same temptations?

Giving into those temptations will never make us content. But we can't withstand them on our own. We desperately need the help of the One who knows how hard it is to resist them. Jesus fought temptation with truth (Matthew 4:1-11), and we can do the same. We'll have to renew our minds again and again if we want to avoid getting swept up into the world's way of doing things. We'll work on that in the next couple of days.

DAY 3

It's difficult to get rid of the notion that contentment is dependent on circumstances. Usually we think, *Well, of course I'd be content if I were in her shoes. She has the good life. I don't.*

So when we're discontent, we don't go to God for help to become content. We go to God for help to change our circumstances. But what if He *doesn't* change our circumstances? And what if we can't change our circumstances? How do we stop longing for the things we don't have—the things we feel we *have* to have in order to be happy?

The answer is simple: We give up our have-to-haves. Jesus showed us the way. He was willing to do anything for the Father and for us. We always think of Jesus suffering when He died on the cross, but He suffered long before He ever got to the cross.

What does Hebrews 2:18 say about Jesus suffering?

_____

Isn't that interesting? Jesus *suffered* when He was tempted. Would it have been easier for Him to give into temptation? Yes, of course. But the easy way isn't always the best way. Often the hard way is the only way if we want to obey God—but it's not our natural inclination.

In Matthew 16:21-28, Peter shows us his attitude toward Jesus having to suffer. Why do you think Peter was so opposed to Jesus's plan?

_____

_____

Jesus responds to Peter by saying, "Get behind me, Satan! You are a stumbling block to me; you do not have in mind the concerns of God, but merely human concerns." (Matthew 16:23)

• Satan is another word for adversary, and we normally think of a stumbling block as something or someone that encourages us to sin. Why do you think Jesus called Peter a stumbling block?

_____

Jesus knew about the suffering that was to come, including His death on the cross. How do you think He felt about it? (See also Hebrews 12:2.)

_____

We have to remember that Jesus was fully God and fully man. I'm sure the man part of Him dreaded the suffering of the cross. Yet He was also God and knew that it needed to be done. Peter was a stumbling block because he wasn't helping Jesus to do what God wanted Him to do. Peter didn't want Jesus to suffer, but Jesus knew he *had* to suffer in order to do the will of God.

• How about us? Do we sometimes have to suffer to do the will of God in our lives? Why or why not?

_____

_____

Unnecessary suffering flies in the face of what our culture teaches these days. Life should be easy, we're told. Why suffer when you don't have to? What does Matthew 16:24 say?

_____

_____

My friend, the situation that you're discontent with may be a cross that you have to bear for Jesus. Yes, you can work on making life more enjoyable, but there are times when "more enjoyable" conflicts with what God wants you to do. At that point anyone who encourages you to go the easy route is actually being a stumbling block to you. Like Jesus, we need to listen to God, not man.

• Our culture tends to embrace the philosophy that life should be easy and fun and that we shouldn't have to suffer. Can you think of any ways that that philosophy has been a stumbling block to you, either now or in the past?

_____

_____

_____

This philosophy can also be a stumbling block to us in the area of eating. We feel like we should be able to eat what-we-want-when-we-want. Our friends agree with us. They don't want to see us suffer, and they may pressure us to join in and have a nice little pig-out session with them.

• What can you do to keep from stumbling in those situations?

_____

_____

_____

In order to experience true contentment, we must give up the idea that we have to have certain things to be happy, including the ability to eat what-we-want-when-we-want. When we give up our have-to-haves, we'll experience firsthand the truth of Matthew 16:25, *Whoever loses His life for my sake will find it*, and Matthew 6:33, *Seek first His kingdom and His righteousness, and all these things will be added to you*. Can we do this in our own strength? No way.

What does Philippians 4:13 say?

_____

Notice that it doesn't say, "I can do all things through determination, hard work, and a positive attitude." There are areas in each of our lives that only God can change. If we want to experience victory in those areas, we must rely on God's strength by searching His Word and seeking His face for help with our problems.

Sometimes God changes us in an instant. But more often than not, we have to work at it. We learn to be like Him as we spend time in His Word and apply its truth to our lives.

What does Paul say about how he came to be content in Philippians 4:11?

For I have _____ *to be content in whatever circumstances I am.*

Philippians 4:12 is another enlightening verse. What situations did Paul have to learn to be content in?

_____

_____

Why do you think Paul had to learn to be content in abundance?

_____

_____

When we've been blessed with much, it's easy to begin relying on our own resources. We forget that God is everything, and we turn to other things for fulfillment. But things will never satisfy. When we rely on the blessings rather than the "Blesser," we never have enough blessings to be satisfied. Discontentment is our constant companion.

Laying down our have-to-haves isn't easy. We think we're giving up happiness and any hope of ever being happy. What we're really doing, though, is taking another step toward the intense joy that accompanies a submissive, mind-altering relationship with the Living God.

There is joy on the other side of submission, but we have to take those first painful steps of giving up our own picture of the way life has to be in order to get there. It's not easy, but we can do all things through Him who strengthens us.

DAY 4

Last week, we looked at three questions that could help us let go of our worries. Let's try those questions with discontentment to see how they would help us let go of our unhappiness and embrace life in its "as is" condition.

Do I need to change the way I think?

Sometimes when I'm feeling discontent, I make a chart. On the left I list the culture's perspective (which is usually what I'm buying into at the time), and on the right I list the biblical perspective. When I see the two different views side by side, it's easier to take off the cultural perspective and put on God's perspective.

Why don't you give that a try right now? Compare what the world says about life with what God says about life. Look at the chart on the next page, and finish filling it in by writing down what you think God would say in the right column. If you can think of any Bible verses that apply, add those. If you need help, you can see what I wrote on page 161.

World	God
Life should be fun.	
I deserve to be happy.	
I shouldn't have to work this hard—life should be easy.	
I need to find my soul mate in order to be happy.	
If only I had a (bigger house, nicer car, skinnier body, different boyfriend, better job, etc.), then I would be happy.	
I can't be happy if I'm not living my passion.	

Sometimes we get so caught up in life that it helps to take a breather and say, "Wait a minute—is this really the way I'm supposed to live?" Making a chart like this helps to get a biblical perspective of life.

It also helps us become more content. Because here's the truth: If we think like the world thinks, we'll only be content if we're one of those people out there who has it all together. Wait a minute. There *are* people out there who have it all together, right? Or is that also a lie?

When I feel like my life is getting out of focus, I'll often make a chart like the one you just filled out. It helps me remember what is real and true when I'm bombarded with what the world thinks is right and necessary.

Truth journaling also helps me when I'm discontent. Let's look at a couple of examples of truth journaling for this emotion. I'll do the first one, and you can try the second one.

Journaling Example

Situation: Karen is a working mom who is getting burnt out with the constant demands on her time.

Emotions: Discontent, unhappy

Beliefs: *1. Life is so boring. 2. All I ever do is work—work at work and work at home. 3. If only I didn't have to work, then I would be happy.*

Truth: *1. True 2. I don't actually work all the time. It just feels like all the time. 3. Even if I didn't work, I would still be unhappy at times. Working or not working doesn't make a person happy or unhappy. Only God can bring satisfaction.*

As you can see, Karen was believing some lies. Truth journaling would help her see that she doesn't need the perfect circumstances to make her happy. She only needs God.

Karen could further help her situation by doing an options chart. There is often a practical solution available to a problem, but it's important to have your mind tuned in to God before you start looking at other options.

I'll let you try journaling the next scenario. The interesting thing is that both women are having similar emotions and thoughts even though they're in completely different situations. You can see my journal entry for this example in Appendix B.

Journaling Example

Situation: Beth is a stay-at-home mom with small kids who has spent the day listening to her two year old and four year old fight with the baby crying in the background.

Emotions: Discontent, unhappy

Beliefs: *1. Life is so boring 2. All I ever do is change diapers and break up fights. 3. If only I had a job, then I would be happy.*

Truth:

_____

_____

_____

_____

_____

How did that go? Have you truth journaled enough now that it's getting easier to do? As you renew your mind on a regular basis, you'll begin to notice your reactions changing. You'll believe the truth first time around, and this will affect the way you feel and the way you act.

Is this time consuming? Yes. I might journal a situation today, bring my thoughts captive to the truth, and then experience the exact same thing tomorrow. But if I am faithful to bring my thoughts to the truth each time, I *will* change. There will come a day when that same situation will pop up, and I'll react with compassion instead of anger or with contentment rather than dissatisfaction. I encourage you to take the time to truth journal. God will use it to change your life on a deep level.

Do I need to act?

Sometimes the only thing you can change in a difficult situation is your attitude, but other times you may be able to take action. Here's an example. Let's say I'm discontent because my kids are running wild and driving me crazy. What could I do to solve this problem?

_____

I'm hoping you said, "Discipline the kids," and not, "Put the kids in front of the television and have a bowl of ice cream!" In this situation, it would actually be very important to act—both for the welfare of the mom and the kids.

What do you think would keep a mom from acting in a situation like this?

_____

The answer to this question would determine what the mom needs to work on. She may have to back up and change her beliefs before she is free to act. For example, maybe she hasn't disciplined the kids because she thinks that would stifle their creativity or independence. This might be the current parenting philosophy but she would have to ask herself, "Does this agree with God's philosophy?" What do you think?

_____

There is plenty of support for self-control and discipline in the Bible and not so much support for kids running wild! This mom will have a much better chance of successfully disciplining her kids if she actually believes that it's good for them to be disciplined.

Another reason a mom might not act in a situation like this is that it's *hard* to act. Sure, it's not easy to watch the kids jump off the walls, but it may be easier than going to all the work of trying to train them to be different. In this case, a mom might have to work on the belief that she actually *can* make a difference through discipline and that it's worth the effort.

In both cases it will take a lot of hard work to change the situation, but there will be a better chance for success if the mom works on her beliefs first.

• Why do you think she'll have a better chance for success if she works on her beliefs first?

_____

_____

Think of a situation you're discontent with. Is there any action you need to take?

_____

_____

Are there any beliefs you need to change first in order to make it easier to act?

_____

_____

Another action you can take when you're discontent is to spend some time in praise and thanksgiving. Make a long list of what you have to be thankful for. Spend some time in prayer, thanking God for who He is and what He's done in your life. Turn on some praise music, lie down on the couch, and worship Him as you listen to the music. It always surprises me how much my attitude changes when I focus on what I have, rather than on what I don't have. It's a great cure for discontentment.

Do I need to submit?

Submission. It seems unAmerican, doesn't it? We'd rather just keep working until we find some other way to fix the problem! It's hard to acknowledge the fact that sometimes you just have to accept an unpleasant situation.

• Why do you think we have such a difficult time submitting to unpleasant situations? (Again, I'm not suggesting we submit to truly abusive situations.)

_____

_____

Have you ever felt that, by submitting yourself to a disagreeable situation, you were condemning yourself to a life of unhappiness? And that the only reason you were submitting to it was that you had run out of ideas to change it?

God wants us to be content in *any* situation. Often the only thing we can change about a situation is our attitude, especially when that situation involves other people. It would be nice to have a magic wand that we could wave over the problem people in our lives to shape them up, but God hasn't given us that power. Instead we need to forgive them and accept them and give them grace. Just like we hope they'll do for us.

This isn't easy. The only way we can do it is to go to God again and again to see them from *His* perspective. God is faithful, and He'll meet all our needs. Sometimes, though, we must lay down our lives in submission to Him before we can experience His provision.

Submission is saying, "Lord, I don't like this situation, but I'm willing to do anything for you. If this is what you have for me than *I accept it*. Do with me what you will. I'm your willing servant."

This is different than saying, "Lord, I can't stand this situation. You can see how miserable I am. I can't believe I have to put up with this, but I can't see any way out of it, so I guess I will."

True submission brings peace and joy. Counterfeit submission just sets us up for further disappointment because we're still holding onto our have-to-haves. It's hard to fathom because it's so counter-cultural, but the more we're willing to live any sort of life for God, the happier we are.

DAY 5

Today, we'll talk about boredom. This is one of the most common motivations for eating when we're not hungry. There are two reasons we get bored: either we have nothing to do, or we have a lot to do but it's all boring. We'll spend the majority of the lesson on the first type of boredom and cover the second type at the end of the lesson.

• Let's begin by looking at the culture's answer to boredom. If you have time on your hands, how does the world say you're supposed to fill it?

I would be curious to see your answers. It kind of depends on who your world is, right? Some will say, "Find a hobby." Others will say, "Get a job," and still others will say, "Go do something fun!" And while there is nothing wrong with doing any of those things, when our minds immediately jump to filling our time with things that will make us happy, we're missing out on one of the main messages in the Bible. Let's take a look at that message.

Read Mark 10:35-45. What kind of life is Jesus asking His disciples to live?

• What's the difference between the lifestyle the world tells us to live and the lifestyle Jesus tells us to live?

_____

_____

• Now back up a bit and read Mark 10:32-34, 45. What kind of life did Jesus live, and why do you think He lived that way? When you answer this question, think not only of his death, but also of the way he lived his life while on earth.

_____

_____

What would you need to change about your life to make it more like Jesus's life?

_____

_____

Would it be hard to live a life of service? Why or why not?

_____

_____

Living our lives to serve others is a foreign concept to most of us. In a "Look out for Number One" world, it often doesn't even cross our minds to serve others. When we do think of serving them, we feel like we should be rewarded for our efforts—if not financially, then at least with gratefulness on their part.

Do you think Jesus felt like everyone was grateful for His efforts to serve them when He lived on earth and when He died on the cross? Why or why not?

_____

What was Jesus's motivation for serving us? (John 3:16, 1 John 3:16)

_____

Let's read another passage and explore this idea further. Read Luke 10:25-37 and answer the questions below.

What did Jesus say is the most important commandment?

_____

What is the second most important commandment?

_____

In what ways did the Samaritan have to sacrifice to love the man in this story well?

_____

_____

Why do you think the other people in this story didn't stop to help the injured man?

_____

• When we're bored, why do you think service to others isn't the first thing on our list of things to do?

_____

Jesus tells us to love our neighbors. He then goes on to tell us who our neighbors are: anyone we're in a position to help. The traveler on the road in this parable needed help, and the Samaritan was in a position of being able to help him. Can you think of any "neighbors" in your life that could use your help?

_____

_____

If you have time on your hands, you have a great resource that God can use. Look around to see who needs help in your church or community. Look around to see what type of ministries are available. Check with your community volunteer agency. There are all kinds of exciting opportunities to minister to people in your local community.

If you were to serve one person in your life this week, whom would you serve and how would you serve them?

_____

If you have extra time on your hands, list a few ministries or volunteer activities you might like to get involved in. What is the first step you'd have to take if you wanted to get involved in one of those opportunities?

_____

How are you feeling about all of this? Are you thinking that life will be really humdrum if you adopt an attitude of service? Actually, I think life will be more exciting than ever if you live the way God wants you to live. If you're ministering in the area of your gifts and desires, you'll probably have a lot of fun as you minister. God will bless you as you bless others.

Now let me say a word to those of you who don't have much free time, but still find yourself bored. I know how hard it is to live in a boring situation if you're a person who craves excitement. Everything in us wants to get out there and have fun and our tendency is to do whatever we can to escape the boredom, if not physically, then at least mentally.

But here's the question we need to ask ourselves in those situations: *Has God called me to this situation? Is it a situation I need to be in right now?* If the answer is yes, then we need to submit to God and stay there. Sometimes life is boring! That's okay. God can use bored. And He can also change bored. As you run to Him for help with life, He will help you become more content.

When I look back on life, it's often those difficult periods of my life that I'm most thankful for because I can see how God used them for my good. Don't leave a situation God has placed you in just because it's not exciting. Instead, do what you can to liven it up, and accept the rest. God will use the situation for your good.

If you're in a boring situation, can you think of anything God might want to teach you through this trial?

_____

_____

• If you struggle with boredom, can you think of any practical things you can do to liven up your life while you're in your current situation? If you're doing this Bible study with a group, why don't you share your ideas with each other?

_____

_____

_____

My friend, any life can be a good life if we're living it for God and with God. In closing, record Paul's words in Philippians 1:21. Let that be our attitude!

_____

_____

Anger

Mary was fed up. The company had downsized and now she was expected to do the work of two people. "How do they expect me to do it all?" she thought. She knew very well how they expected her to do it—more unpaid overtime. They didn't seem to think she had a life apart from work. Oh well, she thought, at least I'm home in time for dinner. She pulled into the garage, grabbed her briefcase, and walked in on a scene of utter chaos. The house was a mess, the kids were wrestling, and Bill was sitting in front of the television. "Hi, honey," he said. "What's for dinner?"

We don't lack for opportunities to be annoyed, do we? When we're angry, we usually think it's the other person's fault. *If only he wasn't so lazy,* we think, *then I wouldn't be angry.* Or, *Of course, I'm annoyed. Who wouldn't be annoyed in this situation?*

What we don't realize is that anger is often a response to pain. Husbands are inconsiderate. Friends are indifferent. Children rebel. And we respond to all of them with annoyance. Even when what we really are is hurt.

Although anger is usually triggered by the behavior of others, it's often our response to their behavior that's the problem. In this chapter we'll talk about learning how to forgive and let go of those angry feelings.

If you have an ongoing relationship where you are consistently angry, use the ideas in this chapter to learn how to forgive and let go of anger, but also consider seeing a counselor to discuss the relationship and look for ways to improve it. It's possible that you may be able to add some boundaries to that relationship or come up with some other practical solutions that will help the relationship.

It's also important to see a counselor if you can't let go of your angry feelings, especially if you've been covering them up with food. When you stop using food to cope with the problem, you may experience your emotions at a more intense level. Your feelings of anger may surprise you. Please seek professional help if you need it.

This week we'll look at the negative impact of anger on our own lives and the lives of others. We'll explore the attitude God wants us to have toward the sins of others and discuss some ways to get over our angry feelings.

DAY 1

Today we'll look at the negative impact of anger on our own lives and on the lives of those around us. James 1:19-20 lists one reason why we're to be slow to anger. What is it?

_____

• God wants us to be righteous. How does our anger hinder His work in our lives?

_____

Do you think being swift to hear and slow to speak have anything to do with anger? If so, what?

_____

Anger often comes in response to a trial. We're involved with a difficult person or unfair situation, and we become annoyed. *This isn't fair*, we shout. Instead of submitting to God, we rush to blame other people. We're innocent; they're to blame.

When our eyes are on the faults of others, they're not on God. We're so busy being annoyed with the other person that we're not open to God working in our lives.

If we instead turn to Him in the difficult situation, He can use it to change us in ways that bring about righteousness, both in our own lives as we submit to Him, and in the lives of others as they see our godly response.

• Can you think of a time in your life when your anger hindered God from working? What could He have developed in you had you submitted to Him instead?

_____

_____

• Anger can also prevent righteousness in the lives of the people we're angry with. This may sound far-fetched but think about it for a moment. Who would be more likely to influence your attitude and behavior in a positive way? A friend who gently and lovingly explains how you've hurt him or her, or a friend who angrily throws your faults in your face? Explain.

_____

_____

• Have you ever been in a situation where someone was angry with you? What was your first reaction?

_____

Often we look at angry people as the "bad guys." We get defensive when they criticize, and we're upset with them for being so nasty. Our efforts focus on appeasing their anger, trying to live up to their expectations, or avoiding them altogether. We may even get angry ourselves and begin to dislike them.

What probably won't happen is an honest look at ourselves before God to see if there's anything He wants to change in our lives. We're so focused on the other person's anger and what *they* think of us that we forget to ask God to see what *He* thinks of our behavior. In this case, the anger of the other person can hinder the work of the Holy Spirit in our lives.

Another reason we need to be careful with anger is that it's so easy to let anger slip into judgment and condemnation. Paul talks about this in Romans 14:1-13. In these verses, the Christians are judging each other because of different beliefs about food. I'm sure you've all experienced church disputes where people take sides about debatable issues. People tend to get angry in those situations.

What does God want our attitude to be when we disagree with each other? (Romans 14:10,13)

_____

Why are we not supposed to judge other people? (Romans 14:4)

_____

Do you ever worry about what the other person's getting away with? It helps to remember that the person we're angry with is God's responsibility. Someday they'll have to answer to God for their actions, but God doesn't call them to answer to us!

What attitude does Jesus want us to have toward the sins of others? (Luke 6:36-42)

_____

We must be very careful with our anger. If God is merciful, who are we to be unmerciful? Do you see how presumptuous that is? We desperately need to forgive. He requires it of us.

Ephesians 4:26-27 lists another danger of anger. What is it?

_____

Can you think of a time in your life when unresolved anger gave a place for Satan to work in your life? What did it lead to?

_____

_____

Unresolved anger can lead to resentment, condemnation, and even hatred. It hurts our relationship with God and poisons our relationships with other people. We must deal with our anger as soon as possible so Satan doesn't get a foothold in our lives. In fact, it's so important that God gives us a boundary in Ephesians 4:26. How soon are we supposed to resolve our anger?

_____

The question is, how do we get rid of those angry feelings? Sometimes the other person doesn't want to talk about the problem. Or they're willing to talk, but they're not willing to change. The situation seems hopeless, and we're stuck with our angry feelings. We'd like to forgive, but we don't know how.

Here's the interesting thing: Paul has already told us how to get rid of those angry feelings. Back up just a few verses and read Ephesians 4:22-25. Remember those verses from pages 19-20 of this study? According to those verses, what do you need to do if you want to get rid of your angry feelings and forgive?

_____

_____

Remember that what we *think* determines what we feel. So if we're thinking horrible thoughts about that person who just hurt us, we'll continue to be angry. The only way to get rid of the anger is to see the situation and the person through God's eyes. When we take the time to renew our minds, it's easier to let go of our angry feelings and forgive the person.

As we study this more during the week, try to remember that it's God's responsibility to change people; our responsibility is to love them. He never said that living the gospel would be easy, did He?

DAY 2

The world tells us we have a right to be angry when people aren't treating us well. We deserve better! Yet God thinks differently. He gave us grace, and He wants us to give grace to others.

I like this definition of grace: *unmerited favor.* Unmerited means that the person doesn't deserve our favor. He did nothing to earn it. What he probably *deserves* is our anger. But God wants us to give him grace instead. To love him unconditionally and forgive him.

That doesn't mean we can't do anything to change an unpleasant situation. What it means is that we evaluate our options based on God and His Word, not on our feelings and our "rights."

What does Paul say we are to pursue in Romans 14:19?

_____

_____

When we're angry with someone, our biggest enemy is our mouth. What tends to come out of our mouths when we're upset?

_____

_____

• Do the things we naturally want to say edify the other person and lead to peace? If not, what do they do?

_____

_____

_____

Romans 14:20 says, *Do not tear down the work of God for the sake of food.* This verse is part of the passage we discussed yesterday regarding the differences of opinion the church was having about what to eat. What it's really saying is this: *Don't tear down the other person just because you don't agree with him.*

But what if it's not just a disagreement? What if the other person has really wronged you? Let's look at Ephesians 4:29-32. According to this passage, how should we respond to others?

_____

_____

_____

• We need the Word of God stored in our hearts if we're to have the right attitude towards others. On the following chart, I've listed some beliefs we've learned from the world that aren't biblical. Read the verse indicated and record the truth on the right.

World	God
I need to give her a piece of my mind. Ephesians 4:29	
He's a jerk. Psalm 139:13-14	
I deserve to be treated well. Philippians 2:3-8	
He can't get away with that! Romans 15:1, 7	

We need to remember that God hasn't given us the responsibility or the power to change others. Sure, we can say something in kindness to let them know how their behavior hurts us. But if they're not open to change, we need to step back and let the Holy Spirit go to work on them.

Remember Romans 14:4? They're answerable to God, not to us. He asks us to forgive them and pray for them, not resent them and be mean to them. Jesus is our example. He had ample opportunity to be angry with those who mistreated Him while He lived on earth.

What did He do instead? (Philippians 2:5-8)

_____

• What would this attitude look like in your own life in response to the person with whom you're angry?

_____

_____

That's hard to swallow, isn't it? You can see why we would need to renew our minds in order to have the strength to follow through with it. We may think we can't be happy unless the other person changes, but God can give us peace and joy in any situation if we rely on Him.

• Why does God want us to forgive each other and not demand our own way all the time? (Romans 15:1-7)

_____

_____

Are you having a hard time believing that you can actually stop being angry with someone who is driving you crazy? Are you having a hard time even *wanting* to forgive them?

Remember that what is impossible for man is possible for God. He can do anything, including healing our relationships. We'll spend the rest of the week learning how to get rid of those angry feelings so we can love people the way God wants us to love them.

DAY 3

When other people sin against us, we have a choice. Will we forgive them, or will we hold a grudge? If we cling to our resentment, we'll begin to feel distant from God. He gives us grace when we don't deserve it, and He wants us to give that same grace to others when they don't deserve it.

But how do you turn off the feelings? You may want to forgive them in theory, but how do you let go of the anger? The Bible has answers for everything, and it has an answer for this.

Today's Bible passage in Philippians will help us retrain our minds. It will show us how to rightly think about the people who make us so angry. Read this passage over a couple of times and then we'll discuss it.

Finally, brethren, whatever is true, whatever is honorable, whatever is right, whatever is pure, whatever is lovely, whatever is of good repute, if there is any excellence and if anything worthy of praise, dwell on these things. The things you have learned and received and heard and seen in me, practice these things, and the God of peace will be with you. Philippians 4:8-9 (NASB)

Now did Paul really have to be so wordy? Couldn't he just have said, "Think positive"? Since they didn't have copy machines in those days and it took so much effort to copy the Scriptures word for word, we have to believe that Paul had a purpose for each word he used in this passage.

Paul tells us in verse 8 to dwell on these things. The Greek word used for dwell is *logizomai*. The essence of the word means to reason or reckon. It's not just a thought popping into your head, but a thought that's come by way of careful reasoning. We're supposed to spend some time really thinking about these things.

Let's try that with today's passage. We'll go through Paul's words one at a time with a specific person in mind, preferably one that annoys you. Before you read any further, get a sheet of paper so you can write down your thoughts as you go. Dwell on what is good in that person by applying each word to them. If you have a problem with anger, this will really help.

True

Do you think it's significant that truth is the first item on the list? We begin by renewing our minds! Are you believing any lies that are making you angry with this person? If you begin by truth journaling, you'll clear up a few problems right away. This gives you the right mindset to go through the rest of the list. Why don't you go ahead and try that now, and then we'll move on to the next word in Paul's list.

Honorable

A person who is honorable has integrity and strong moral character. He is honest, ethical, and worthy of respect. Is there anything honorable about the person you're angry with? Anything about him that you respect? Also, are you being honorable in the way that you think of him? Are you being honorable in the way that you talk about him with your friends? How can you honor him in your thoughts and actions? Go ahead and answer those questions and then we'll move on to the next word.

Right

This word comes from the Greek word *dikaios* which is usually translated righteous or just. Is there anything righteous or just about this person? Have you been just in your evaluation of him? Are you only looking at his faults and not his strengths? Are you seeing this person through God's eyes? Is it "right" to think of him as a jerk?

Pure

Are you having pure thoughts toward this person? If not, are you filling your mind with anything that is causing those impure thoughts? For example, romance novels, even Christian ones, can have a negative effect on your mind if they cause you to think impure things. Many women choose not to read romances because they start expecting their husbands to be like the perfect man in the book. Remember, we are to guard our thoughts like a jailer guards his prisoners. That's pretty drastic. Is there anything you need to change so you can protect your thoughts toward this person?

Lovely

The Greek word for lovely is an interesting word. The word is *prosphilees,* and it's made up of two smaller words, *pros,* which means towards, and *philees,* which means friend, so the literal translation would be "toward friends." Does this person have any qualities that make her a good friend? Is there anything lovely about her?

Of Good Repute

The Greek word used here is *euphaima,* another compound word that literally means "well said." What good things do other people say about this person? What good things is he known for?

Excellence

The Greek word used for excellence refers to moral excellence or virtue. What virtues does this person have? What are her moral standards? Does she have any natural areas of moral excellence? Any areas where she has grown significantly?

Worthy of Praise

The Greek word used for praise here usually refers to accomplishments. Is there anything he is really good at? Any areas of giftedness? Has he accomplished any great things?

If you tend to be a critical person, going through this verse word by word with a person who annoys you in mind will help you turn your thoughts around. There are always two sides to each person: weakness and strength. We choose which side to dwell on.

When it comes to how we view other people, we need to use the criteria of God's Word and the measuring stick of God's grace rather than the criteria of the world and the measuring stick of perfection.

If you tend to focus on the faults of others, I would encourage you to pray for them. God may have given you a gift of discernment, but He wants you to use it to pray for people, not to be annoyed with them.

Praying for them will not only help to bring about change in *their* lives, but it will also help to bring about change in your own life. As you learn to accept and love people in their "as is" condition, God will be changing you so that you reflect His character. Thank God for the annoying habits of other people because He can use them to get rid of our own annoying habits!

DAY 4

Do you ever find yourself constantly annoyed, even with the ones you love? Anger is one of those emotions that can drive us crazy. Not only does it make us unhappy, it also hurts our relationships—because people don't like it when we're always annoyed with them.

If you struggle with anger, it will help to discover why you're angry. Usually, we think we're angry because of the other person's behavior. In truth, much of our anger is caused by our own unrealistic expectations, beliefs, and desires.

Today and tomorrow, we'll look at four different reasons for anger. If you can understand why you're angry, it will be easier to let go of it. Here are the four reasons we'll be studying:

I will get angry if ...

1. I'm expecting another person to make me happy.
2. I don't think I should have to suffer.
3. I have unrealistic expectations for others.
4. I care too much about what others think.

Let's go over each of these in depth.

Expecting Others to Make Us Happy

Have you ever felt that you couldn't be happy in your present circumstances? Maybe there's someone at work who is making your life miserable. Or your spouse isn't meeting your needs. Or your roommate is getting on your nerves.

It's easy to blame others for our unhappiness. If only they were different, *then* we would be happy. Yet they aren't different. They do the same annoying things, over and over, and there is nothing we can do to stop them.

Anger frequently comes in situations we have no control over. It may be a situation we can't change, or it may be a situation we can't change with a clear conscience.

When this happens, we only have one option that will lead to peace: We need to give up the picture that's roaming around inside our heads of the way life has to be. In other words, accept life and people in their "as is" condition. When we do that, with our heart as well as our behavior, God more than meets our needs.

Read Jeremiah 31:13-14. What can the Lord do for you in the midst of your unhappiness?

_____

The last part of Jeremiah 13:14 gives us a clue as to how God changes our hearts when we submit to Him. Notice it says that we will be satisfied with His goodness (some versions say bounty or good gifts).

The situations we're in may not change. But God can bring wonderful things into our lives that we never even imagined, all because we were willing to give up the things we thought we had to have to be happy. We will be satisfied with *His* goodness.

That's not all that happens, though. God also uses those difficult people in our lives to change us in ways that we need to change.

Think of a difficult person in your own life. Can you think of anything God might want you to learn through your relationship with that person?

_____

How do you think God wants you to respond to that person?

_____

• What will happen to your character if you submit to the Lord and respond the way He wants you to respond, with your heart as well as your actions?

_____

• What will happen to your character if you don't submit to God and instead hold onto your anger?

_____

Holding on to anger can lead to resentment, bitterness, and even hatred. It can spill over into all areas of our lives, turning us into negative people who aren't fun to be around.

Learning to accept people in their "as is" condition and give grace is life-changing. It opens up a whole new realm of relationship opportunities because we're suddenly free to enjoy all sorts of people, even people who used to get on our nerves. People enjoy us more too as we become less critical, less demanding, and more loving.

But the best benefit of all is what letting go of our anger does for our relationship with God. He wants us to forgive, and when we say no, it causes a rift between us. When we say yes, we grow closer to God as we share in the fellowship of His suffering (Philippians 3:7-10) and cling to Him for help in loving well.

The relationship we need to cultivate with the Lord can be found in Psalm 63:1-8. How would you describe David's relationship with God?

_____

• How would it change your life and your relationships if you had this sort of bond with God? Or, if you already have this sort of relationship with God, how has it already changed your life?

_____

_____

Cultivating a close, dependent relationship on God is the best thing you can do if you want to have healthy and enjoyable relationships with the difficult people in your life. If He's meeting all of your needs, you'll be less inclined to get angry when others don't meet them. Let's take a look at another reason we tend to get angry with difficult people.

Thinking We Shouldn't Have to Suffer

When we feel like we shouldn't have to put up with hardship, it will annoy us when others inconvenience us. Here's an example. Let's say I'm at the Department of Motor Vehicles, waiting in line to renew my driver's license. The woman ahead of me is just chatting away with the clerk and is taking *forever* to finish her business.

If my normal approach to life is that I shouldn't have to suffer, I'll be extremely irritated with that woman. After all, she's inconveniencing me, and I shouldn't have to put up with it.

I'll be far more content if I change my attitude and accept the fact that life isn't always easy, and it's arrogant of me to expect it to be. The truth is, we're a bit spoiled. We want what we want when we want it. And when others get in the way of what we want, we become annoyed.

What do you think God would say about this attitude of ours? (Philippians 2:3-8, James 1:2-4)

_____

God allows trials in our lives to mature us. The culture might say we deserve an easy life, but God doesn't say that. In fact, if we're believing this lie, then God will probably allow frustrating situations—and people—into our lives to help us get over this selfish belief.

Think of a difficult person in your own life. What would it look like to love this person with a Philippians 2:3-8 sort of love?

_____

_____

_____

Unrealistic Expectations for Others

Another reason we become annoyed with others is because they fail to live up to our expectations for them. This is a common source of anger for both the person who has a highly developed sense of right and wrong and for the perfectionist.

Here are some examples of this kind of anger: getting mad at your husband or roommate because they aren't as clean as you want them to be, getting mad at the people in your church or Bible study because they're not as involved as you want them to be, or getting mad at a friend because she often makes plans with you and then cancels them.

If you want to stop being annoyed, stop asking the question, "What *should* this person do?" and start asking the question, "What can I expect this person to do?"

When we continually expect people to be different than they've already shown themselves to be, we're choosing to live in the land of disappointment.

Since we can't change others, it's much better to give up our unrealistic expectations for their behavior and just get over it. Give them grace. Love them. Forgive them. Accept them—faults and all. After all, isn't that what we're hoping they'll do for us?

When we get annoyed with people on a regular basis, it's easy to slip into judgment mode. What does God say about judgment in Matthew 7:1-5?

_____

_____

You may find that the expectations you put on other people aren't even God's expectations. They're just the way *you* think things should be done. But people are different. They have different interests, different personalities, and different ways of living life. And they don't need to live up to our expectations for them. You may find, on the other hand, that the person you're angry with isn't just doing things differently. She's actually sinning.

What is your responsibility if the person sinning is a Christian? (Luke 17:3)

_____

It's difficult to rebuke people or talk seriously about things they've done to hurt us. We don't want to hurt their feelings or have them get mad at us. Instead, our tendency is to make a joke about it or avoid them for a while. This often hurts our relationships, and it may keep others from growing in ways that God wants them to grow.

If you're going to rebuke someone—or even if you're not rebuking, but just bringing up something that bugs you—make sure you renew your mind first. The other person will be far more receptive to what you have to say if she senses that you love and accept her. The judgment, pride, and annoyance questions and Bible verses in *I Deserve a Donut* will help you prepare your mind if you need help.

Once you've brought the matter up, don't forget to leave it in God's hands, especially if the person isn't receptive to your ideas. God can change anyone. But the person you're annoyed with may not want to change. Or they may want to change and not know how to change. Or they may be working on change—and even going to God for help to change—but it's taking awhile.

We can help people who want to be helped, but if we keep trying to help people who don't want to be helped, they'll just become annoyed with us and it will lead to division. If you're in one of those situations, ask a wise friend or counselor for advice, and go to God for help in loving and accepting this person in her "as is" condition.

The truth is, we're all sinners. We shouldn't be surprised when others do and say things that hurt and annoy us, because we do and say things that hurt and annoy others. God gives *us* grace when we're jerks. Shouldn't we also give others grace?

DAY 5

Yesterday we looked at three reasons for anger. We said that we tend to get angry when we're expecting others to make us happy, when we feel like we shouldn't have to suffer, and when we have unrealistic expectations for others. Today we'll look at one last reason for our angry feelings: caring too much about what others think.

Caring Too Much About What Others Think

If I feel like people *have* to think well of me, I'll become angry or upset when people criticize me, when I think they don't like me, or when someone in my family does something to embarrass me. It's natural to want others to think well of us, but we get in trouble when we *need* others to think well of us.

• Why do you think we get so upset when others criticize us, get annoyed with us, judge us, or condemn us in some way?

_____

_____

Let me ask you something. Is everything that you do worthy of respect? Is it possible for your kids (or friends) to behave well in public all of the time? Is it possible for *you* to behave well in public all the time?

We kid ourselves if we think people are going to approve of everything we do. The truth is that we are going to mess up, our kids are going to mess up, and other people are going to mess up. No one is going to think well of us all the time! The only way to escape this compulsion to live for the approval of others is to see ourselves through God's eyes.

Read the following verses and record what they say about who we are.

Genesis 1:27_____

Genesis 1:31_____

Psalm 139:1-6, 13-14_____

_____

Romans 3:23 _____

Romans 8:1_____

Ephesians 2:10_____

1 John 3:1-2_____

There's no use basing our self-esteem on being "good enough," because we're *not* good enough. We're sinners. If people think there's something wrong with us, they're right! There's something wrong with us.

Yet God loves us. We're precious to Him, and He likes the way He made us. We don't have to measure up to the standards of the world to be acceptable because we're acceptable to the One who made the world.

Why don't we try to truth journal a couple of examples about living up to expectations? We'll start with Sue. Let's say that Sue's mother is very critical. Lately she's been getting on Sue about her weight, and it's really bugging Sue.

I'll record what Sue might write in her journal, and then you can record the truth for each thought. You'll have to use your imagination since Sue is a hypothetical person, but it will be good practice in journaling. You can see what I wrote after you finish writing yours.

Beliefs: *1. All my mom ever does is criticize. 2. Nothing is ever good enough for her. 3. She expects me to be perfect when she isn't perfect herself. 4. She is really getting on my nerves. 5. I wish I had a mom who loved me no matter what.*

Truth:

1._____

_____

2._____

_____

3._____

_____

4._____

_____

5._____

_____

Here's how I would journal this one.

1. This isn't true. My mom also does some very nice things for me.

2. This is probably true. My mom is a perfectionist and she naturally sees the flaws in people. She's like this with other people too, not just me. Thankfully, I'm not defined by who I am in my mom's eyes, but by who I am in God's eyes—and in God's eyes, I'm beautiful (Psalm 139:13-14). If the whole world were to stand up, look at me, and shout in unison, "You're such a loser!" God would look at me and say, "No she's not. She's a work of art (Ephesians 2:10)!!!"

3. Interesting. This is true, but she also expects herself to be perfect and gets upset when she isn't. It's probably not very fun being a perfectionist.

4. True (Note: This is a feeling, not a belief, so you can't really do much with it.)

5. (This is also a feeling, but we'll address it anyway.) The truth is, my mom does love me. She's just a critical mom. We're all sinners, and Mom is one too. I need to love and accept her as she is, critical spirit and all.

Can you see how Sue's anger will start to go away as she truth journals? Sue thought she was angry because her Mom was bugging her about her weight. In reality, she was angry because she was hurt. She felt like her mom would only love her if she were skinny.

Sue's angry feelings will disappear when she realizes that she doesn't need to live up to her mom's expectations, that it's actually sin on her mom's part to have those expectations for her, and that her mom probably *does* love her, but that it's not the end of the world if she doesn't. It's sad—but not the end of the world. She'll probably end the journaling session feeling sorry for her mom, but no longer angry with her.

Typically, when you truth journal the emotion of anger, you'll start out feeling very angry. When you're through truth journaling, you should feel at peace. Often you'll be feeling sorry for the person you were angry with before. If you don't experience peace, you've either missed a lie or you need to take the final step of submission.

In Sue's case, she would need to accept the fact that she has a critical mom. If she truth journals, but is still saying in her heart, "I can't stand having a mom like this," she hasn't submitted to God. She needs to come to the point where she can say this from her heart: "Lord, this is the mom you've given me—I accept her. I'm willing to live any sort of life for you, Lord. Help me to love her."

Now, just for fun, why don't we try truth journaling the situation from Sue's *mom's* point of view? We'll see what she's thinking that's making her so annoyed with Sue's weight.

Beliefs: *1. All Sue ever does is eat. 2. She doesn't even care how she looks. 3. I try to help her and she just gets angry. 4. I might as well not even try anymore. 5. Why can't she be more like her sister?*

Before you judge Sue's mom, remember that we *all* have our sin problems. Critical people are not more sinful than non-critical people. It's just a different sin and often a more visible sin. If you yourself are a critical person, journaling like this can help you to overcome it.

Now, why don't you try to write down the truths for Sue's mom? Don't forget to number your sentences. (There is more room to write on the next page.)

_____

_____

_____

_____

_____

_____

_____

Here's what I would write if I were Sue's mom.

1. Sue does many wonderful things other than eating. She's a great homemaker, a good wife and mom, and a lot of fun. She's a beloved child of God who happens to have a problem with eating too much. I'd much rather her be a good mom to my grandchildren than a skinny person. (Not that skinny people can't be good moms.)

2. It doesn't seem like Sue cares how she looks since she hasn't lost weight, but I can't know that for sure. It's possible that she does care but just isn't able to lose the weight. Forgive me, Lord. It's not my place to judge. Help me be compassionate.

3. True. Hmm, maybe this is a clue that I should stop trying to help. (At this point, I would probably take a little time out to visit with God about the matter and learn all kinds of things. Including the fact that I'm caring about things He doesn't care about.)

4. This is probably true. I can't change Sue. She needs to want to change for herself. And if I keep trying to help her, it will just hurt our relationship.

5. Her sister has her own problems. Being overweight isn't one of them, but she's not perfect. I need to appreciate Sue for who she is.

Do you see how truth journaling can help us accept people in there "as is" condition? The next time you're angry with someone, give truth journaling a try if you haven't tried it already.

It may also be helpful to look back over the lessons from today and yesterday if you have a hard time letting go of your anger. Knowing what your anger stems from will help you get over it. When we eat our anger away, we miss out on opportunities to grow. God wants us to deal with our anger—don't let the sun go down on it!

Stress and Anxiety

Liz glanced at her watch. 5:00 and she still hadn't finished the sales proposal. Reluctantly, she put her things away and walked to the car, mentally running through her schedule for the evening. Pick up Clara at dance, stop at the store to get something for dinner, pick up Brad at baseball, then home for a quick supper with Mark before they all went to church for youth group and Bible study.

She slid into the car and continued her planning. Home from church, help the kids with their homework, finish writing the proposal for the sales meeting, lay out her clothes for work the next day ... oh, no, she thought, I almost forgot. I need to pick up my suit at the dry cleaners. As she eased into traffic, she tried to beat down the panic. I can do this, she thought. Just make it through the week. She made a mental note to pick up some ice cream at the store.

Sometimes life just gets too busy, doesn't it? We get caught up in our jobs and our to-do lists and focus all our energy on *getting things done*. Day after day we go through the motions without stopping to think, *Is what I'm doing really important?*

This week we'll be looking at God's priorities for our lives. We'll see what's important to Him and how it differs from what's important to us. Later on in the week we'll discuss some practical ways to simplify our lives and deal with stress. If you eat when you're stressed, learning how to reduce the stress in your life will be another tool you can use in your battle against emotional eating.

DAY 1

Let's begin by getting a clear picture of our culture. Think of what you see on television, read in magazines, and observe in day-to-day life. What does our culture value?

_____

Now take a look at our own life. What do *you* value?

_____

Now think about how you use all of your time, especially your spare time. Does the way you spend your time reflect what you think is most important in life? If not, what does it say about what's important to you?

_____

_____

For those of us who have kids, looking at what we value in *their* lives can be another way to see what we actually value in our own lives. We may say we want our kids to grow up and love God, but is that where we're putting our efforts?

Are we more concerned with them getting good grades, being involved in sports and music, having friends and being happy, or are we more concerned with them developing godly character? Are we more concerned with them going to youth group each week, or are we more concerned with them meeting with God each day?

Jesus often spoke about what was important in life. In Matthew 19:16-30, a man asked Jesus what he needed to do to obtain eternal life. Jesus said, "Keep the commandments." For some reason, the young man wasn't clear what commandments Jesus was talking about, so he said, "Which ones?" Now this is the interesting part. Which commandments did Jesus give him?

_____

Now look back at the original Ten Commandments in Exodus 20:1-17. Four of the Ten Commandments deal with loving God and six of the Ten Commandments deal with loving others. You probably noticed the same thing I did. Jesus only listed the commandments that had to do with loving one's neighbor.

Why do you think Jesus left out the first four commandments that all dealt with loving God?

_____

Jesus understands human nature so well. I guess that's not surprising considering who He is. Jesus knew that the young man wasn't putting God first in his life so He started with the commandments about loving his neighbors. Apparently the young man was doing well in that category, and he told Jesus so. What gives you a clue that the young man knew that it wasn't enough to just keep those commandments? (Matthew 19:20)

_____

How does Jesus answer him in Matthew 19:21?

_____

• Why do you think Jesus told the young man to sell everything and follow Him? Do you think He requires the same of us? Why or why not?

_____

_____

Can you think of any other situations in the Bible where God asked someone to give up everything and follow Him?

_____

How about Abraham when God asked Him to give up everything and follow Him into a strange land (Hebrews 11:8)? How about Jeremiah when God asked Him to be a prophet to a nation that didn't really want to listen to him (Jeremiah 1)? How about the disciples when Jesus said, "Come, follow me, and I will make you fishers of men?"

God has a history of asking people to give up everything to follow Him. Jesus continued the trend by asking the rich young ruler to give up all his possessions. The young man wanted to follow Jesus but he wasn't willing to make the sacrifice. It was just too hard.

• Do you think the church today emphasizes the message that we have to sacrifice to follow God? If not, what do you think they emphasize and why do you think they emphasize that?

_____

_____

Jesus goes on to talk about how hard it is for a rich man to get into heaven. Now you have to admit, most of us are rich compared to the New Testament poor. We would probably all fall into the "hard to get into heaven" category.

Why do you think it's more difficult for the rich to enter the kingdom of heaven than the poor?

_____

_____

What example did Jesus use to show how difficult this is? (Matthew 19:23-24)

_____

The disciples weren't just astonished at what Jesus had said. They were *greatly* astonished. They thought Jesus was saying that there was no way a rich guy could get into heaven. What did Jesus reply? (Matthew 19:25-26)

_____

I love verse 26: *With man this is impossible, but with God all things are possible.* The Greek word translated "with" is *para*. This preposition has three different meanings in Greek depending on the case of the noun that follows. The meaning in this verse is "in the presence of." So we could say, "In the presence of men, this is impossible, but in the presence of God, all things are possible."

Do you see what Jesus is saying? We can't do it by ourselves. As rich people, we have *so many* pleasant diversions. We're so busy working and playing and having fun and taking care of our belongings that our natural inclination is to push God aside. We think it's normal to schedule Him in for fifteen minutes a day and a couple of hours on Sunday and call ourselves Christians.

But Jesus is saying, "No, you have to be willing to give up everything for me, and you can't do that if you're clinging to the things of the world. You need to be living daily *in my presence*. It's impossible to do without my help."

You see, Jesus knows the temptations that wealth brings. After all, He had been tempted by those things Himself when Satan offered Him the glories of the world (Luke 4:5-6).

Jesus could see that the young man in Matthew cared more about his belongings than he did about God. That's why He asked him to give them up. Putting God first wasn't easy for the rich young man, and it's not easy for us either. We must be very careful not to let the world take hold of us. Our actions and our passions will show what we really love.

I'm afraid normal Christianity has become a practice of *adding* God to our lives rather than *making* Him our life. If this is what we're doing, then we're in dangerous territory.

• Do you think this style of Christianity is acceptable to God? Why or why not?

_____

_____

Think of your own life. What gets in the way of making God first in your life?

_____

_____

What is one thing you could change in your life to live more fully for Him?

_____

_____

We make God first in our lives by giving up our idols, spending time with Him, obeying Him, reading His Word, going to Him for help with our sin, and submitting to His will even when it's not easy or convenient.

We'll never reach the point of perfection, and thanks be to God, we don't need to because we're saved by grace through faith (Ephesians 2:8-9). But we do need to be on the narrow path that leads to Him (Matthew 7:13-14).

In closing today, spend some time in prayer. If God wanted to change one thing in your life, what do you think it would be?

_____

"Therefore I urge you, brethren, by the mercies of God, to present your bodies a living sacrifice, acceptable to God which is your spiritual service of worship." Romans 12:1

DAY 2

It's easy to lose sight of just how much time we need with God each day. If He is to be our provider, our support, our counselor, and our deliverer, then we really need to see Him for more than five or ten minutes each morning.

You can imagine how busy Jesus was at the height of His ministry, yet He still took time to get away from everyone and spend long hours in prayer. If Jesus needed that time to be strengthened, how much more do we need it? Today we'll discuss four reasons why we need to spend time with God. As we get to each reason, fill it in on the lines below.

Reasons to Spend Time with God

1. _____

2. _____

3. _____

4. _____

First, we need to spend time with God in order to develop a close relationship with Him. If I communicate with my husband only five or ten minutes a day on a fairly superficial level, I'm not going to feel close to him. Our emotional intimacy will depend on the quality and quantity of time we spend together. It's the same with God. We shouldn't expect to be excited about our relationship with Him if we don't spend much time with Him.

• Can you think of anything else that hinders emotional intimacy in a relationship with a spouse or a friend?

_____

_____

• Do those same things hurt your relationship with God? In what way?

_____

_____

Another reason we need time with God is to combat the lies Satan likes to throw at us through our involvement with the world. This is what really drew me into a close relationship with God after years of not spending much time with Him. The more He set me free from the lies I was believing, the closer I felt to Him and the more I wanted to spend time with Him and serve Him.

We also need to saturate ourselves with God's presence in order to keep Him first in our lives. It's so easy to let other relationships and activities become more important than our relationship with God. Yet God wants to be first in our lives, not second. We have to be careful not to make idols of the good things in our lives.

Finally, we need to spend time with Him in order to mature. Look with me at a familiar parable in Luke 8:1-8. List below the four places the seed fell and what happened to it in each place.

1._____

2._____

3._____

4._____

Now look at Jesus' explanation of the parable in verses Luke 8:11-15 and share which group of people each seed applies to and what happens to them.

1._____

2._____

3._____

4._____

Which seed do you think most represents the busy lifestyle?_____

What happens to the seed that is choked by life's worries, riches, and pleasures?

_____

The question I need to ask myself is this, "Am I spending enough time with God to mature, or is His influence in my life being choked out by the worries, riches, and pleasures of the world?" In other words, is my relationship with God deep enough to change my bad behavior?

For example, am I less critical today than I was a year ago? Am I more compassionate, less apathetic, more loving, less selfish? If the answer to all of these questions is no, then I'm not spending enough time with God!

We must be careful not to say, "Well, that's just my personality. I have a weakness in that area." God doesn't mean for us to carry those weaknesses to the grave. He wants to transform us!

As I spend time in His Word renewing my mind, He will transform my character. Time is important. If I spend my time the way the world does, then I'll look like the world. If I spend my time the way God wants me to spend it, then I'll begin to look more like Him.

Is there anything in your life that is choking out God's Word? What is it that keeps you from spending more time with Him?

_____

• Are you believing any lies that keep you from spending significant time with Him? If so, what are the lies and what is the truth for each lie?

_____

_____

_____

_____

If you're believing lies that keep you from spending time with God, then it will help to renew your mind before you begin your quiet time each day. Remember that belief creates desire. Believing the truth about time with God will make you *want* to have your quiet times. If discipline isn't your strong suit, then desire is important. God can give you this desire through truth journaling and Scripture prayers.

DAY 3

Brace yourselves, everyone—today we're going to talk about Mary and Martha! The only passage I can think of that produces more groans in a women's Bible study is the one about the wife in Proverbs 31. Let's gather up our courage and turn to Luke 10:38-42, as we can learn a lot from these verses.

First let's get a feel for what's going on. Read the passage and record what the following people are doing:

Jesus_____

Mary_____

Martha_____

Poor Martha. She's feeling overwhelmed with the work, and Mary, an able worker, is just sitting there at the feet of Jesus doing nothing. Does it surprise you that Jesus doesn't encourage Mary to help her sister? Wouldn't most of us parents say, "You're right. Mary, get up and help Martha. She shouldn't have to do all the work herself." But Jesus doesn't say that.

Why do you suppose He didn't make Mary help?

_____

When Mary was sitting at the feet of Jesus, she was obeying the first commandment (Matthew 22:36-39). Jesus was God and she was loving Him with all her heart, soul, and mind by sitting with Him and listening to what He had to say.

Martha didn't see it that way, though. What did she think about Mary's behavior?

_____

I'm sure we can all relate. When you have a million things to do, it's frustrating to see someone just sitting there doing nothing. But here's my question. Do we really have to do those million things? Or do we sometimes just *think* we have to do them? What do you think?

_____

• Martha could have sat down at the feet of Jesus and either postponed dinner or made a less elaborate meal. Do you think that would have been the right thing to do? Why or why not?

_____

Think of your own life. Do you ever skip time with God in the morning because you have too much to do? Or do you ever rush through it so you can get on to other things? If so, how would you need to change your thinking in order to make time with God a priority?

_____

_____

Luke 10:40 states that Martha was distracted with the preparations that had to be made. The Greek word used here is *diakonia*. This is the only verse in the New Testament where it's translated preparations (or service in some translations). Usually it's translated ministry.

Martha's "ministry" was to prepare food for Jesus and the other guests in the house, and she wasn't happy about it. At least she wasn't happy about Mary not helping her.

Do you think Martha's attitude affected her ministry? Why or why not?

_____

_____

What would Martha have needed to do to change her bad attitude?

_____

_____

Maybe if Martha had spent time with Jesus like Mary was doing, her heart would have been better prepared to serve with a good attitude. Unfortunately, she was so caught up in her "ministry" that she didn't have time to spend with Him. My friend, if we're not spending time with God, we're not emotionally in a good place to do ministry anyway. We need that time with Him to prepare our hearts to serve with the right attitude.

According to this passage, what is more important, time spent with God or ministry to others?

_____

I've noticed the importance of keeping God first even in writing this Bible study. At first I thought, *I'll just combine my quiet time with my writing time. When I study the verses that I'm going to write about, that will be my time with God.* It didn't work, though. I soon found myself slipping away from God and not feeling close to Him. I made a commitment at that point to always have my quiet time before I spent any time working on the Bible study, no matter how busy I was.

I need to be going to God every day for *my own* restoration. If I only go to Him as a means to minister to others, it won't be long until I have nothing left to give to others.

Martha *needed* that time with Jesus to renew her heart. She needed to realize that spending time with God was more important than accomplishing things on her to-do list. She also had to accept the fact that Mary wasn't always going to do what she wanted her to do.

Jesus could have performed a miracle and put food on the table, or He could have made Mary help, but He didn't do either. If Martha had gotten what she wanted, there would have been no reason for her to work on her bad attitude and wrong priorities. By not fixing Martha's problem, Jesus gave her an opportunity to grow. The next move was up to Martha. She could submit to the truth Jesus was giving her, or she could continue to stew in her bad feelings toward Mary.

Each time we're in a difficult situation we have a choice. We can either cling to our "rights," or we can give them up and submit to God. The truth is what enables us to go willingly.

Have you ever been in a situation where you had to do an unfair amount of work compared to everyone else? If so, how did it make you feel and how did you respond?

_____

When we're in a situation like that, we have four choices: 1) Serve with a good attitude. 2) Serve with a bad attitude. 3) Stop serving (or simplify it in some way) with an "I'm willing to try a different way of looking at life attitude." 4) Stop serving with a vengeful "Well, fine, if you're not going to serve, I'm not going to serve" attitude.

• Which option or options do you think would be most stressful?

_____

• Which option or options do you think would lead to the most growth in your relationship with God and your character? Why?

_____

_____

• Think of your own life. Which option or options do you tend to gravitate toward, and why do you think you take that option?

_____

_____

• Can you force yourself to take the first or third option? If not, what would you need to do if you wanted to take one of those options? (Romans 12:2) What would be the benefits of taking the first or third options?

_____

_____

The interesting thing is that the best options to reduce stress are usually the best options for our relationship with God as well. If we want to have the strength to take those options, though, we'll need to steep ourselves in the truth (John 8:31) and abide in God's Word—because they're not easy options to take.

Mary is our example. She was abiding in the Word. He was right there in front of her face, in fact. But Martha was so busy doing things that she didn't have time for the Word. The truth is, we need God every day. This isn't a relationship that can rest on past visits.

In closing, read Isaiah 26:3 and record the promise you find in that verse.

_____

DAY 4

When we allow our lives to revolve around work, activities, and a to-do list, we're bound to experience stress. We never seem to have enough time to get everything done that we think needs to be done.

The same holds true when we focus our lives on recreation. We ignore our to-do lists because we'd rather have fun, and the result is stress. We're always rushing around at the last minute trying to get things done, and we're frustrated when work gets in the way of pleasure.

The solution for stress isn't a change of lifestyle. It's a change of heart. Only when we live our lives for God, will we find peace. He wants us to focus our lives on loving Him and loving others, not on getting things done, having fun, or whatever else we may focus it on.

That said, there are some practical things we can do to reduce the stress in our lives. We'll spend the rest of the week discussing those things. Today we'll cover procrastination and perfectionism.

I think it's safe to say that we've all experienced one or the other at some point in our lives. Often it's the perfectionism that causes the procrastination. Because much of the stress in our lives can be linked to one or the other, we'll take a look at both of them.

Perfectionism

Perfectionism is all about expectations: the expectations we have for others, the expectations we think others have for us, and the expectations we have for ourselves. What we're looking for is perfection. What we find is something else. And we think it's not enough.

So we spend our lives trying to change ourselves and others so that we can be happy. We say yes to things because we think others expect us to say yes. We have long to-do lists because we think certain things just have to get done. And we get upset when others don't do their share of the work because it keeps us from reaching our goals. In fact, our lives look a lot like Martha's from yesterday's lesson.

I really think Martha was a perfectionist. She had an idea of what should be happening, and it wasn't happening—which thoroughly annoyed her. According to the Greek, she was "anxious and agitated." The Greek word for agitated is *turbazomai*. Think turbulent.

Is your life ever turbulent when things don't go exactly the way you think they should go? Do you feel like things *have* to be done a certain way? If so, then you're probably a perfectionist. When we set our standards too high, we get stressed because we can't attain them. The standards become a burden.

Read Matthew 11:28-30. How would Martha's life change if she followed this advice?

_____

_____

Jesus tells us to take His yoke upon us and learn from Him. Think of a team of oxen yoked together, pulling a wagon. Do you ever feel like you're "pulling the wagon" all by yourself (taking all the responsibility of life on your own shoulders) and that if you don't keep everything together your world will fall apart? If so, how would your life (and your stress level) change if you were to remember that you're yoked together with Christ and that He's in charge, not you?

_____

_____

You may be striving to be perfect in an area God doesn't even care about. You might say, "Well, what about my testimony?" And I would say, "A peaceful, joyful, loving heart focused on God and others is a much stronger testimony than a person who has a perfect house, perfect body, and a perfect life, but is always stressed out because she's trying to keep everything that way!"

Think of your own life. In what areas are you a perfectionist, if any?

_____

• In what ways does perfectionism add stress to your life?

_____

_____

When we focus on what we think *has* to get done, rather than on what God wants us to do, we risk making an idol of our projects and to-do lists. We become too busy to spend time with God and often too busy to spend time with others as well.

Does your perfectionism ever hurt your relationship with God or keep you from ministering to others or spending time with them? Explain.

_____

_____

Perfectionism can also hurt the ones we love when we have unrealistic expectations for their behavior or when we become irritable because of our stress levels. How has your perfectionism hurt your family and friends?

_____

_____

• How would your life improve if you were able to stop being a perfectionist?

_____

_____

The question is, how do you stop? It's hard to just turn off your mind and say, "I'm not going to let that bother me anymore." If you struggle with perfectionism, only God can set you free.

There are many lies that feed into perfectionism. I'll list some of those lies on the following page. Circle the ones that you believe, and write the truth below each lie. If you need help, look at what I wrote on pages 161-162. As you renew your mind and replace these lies with the truth on a regular basis, you'll be working toward a more peaceful life focused on God and others.

Lies that fuel perfectionism

1. This has to be perfect to be acceptable.

2. I am a failure because I (failed in some way).

3. I can't start this project until (the rest of my life is in order, I know exactly how to do it, I have a large block of time available for it, etc.).

4. If it can't be done well, it's not worth doing.

5. If I'm perfect, people will love me, admire me, accept me, etc. If I mess up, they'll be mad at me.

6. It's terrible if I make a mistake.

7. People expect that of me. I need to live up to their expectations.

8. If I want something done right, I need to do it myself.

9. I'm a bad Christian if (I don't go on a short-term missions trip, I'm not a bubbly person, I don't lead a Bible study, I'm not perfect, etc.).

10. I should have known better.

Truth is the answer to the lies of perfectionism. If you're still convinced that perfectionism is a good thing in your life, do some Internet research on the topic. It will open your eyes to the problems of perfectionism.

Before we leave this subject, I'd like to briefly discuss the added temptation we have as Christians in this area. There's a fine line to walk between trying to please God and feeling like He'll be mad at us if we're not perfect.

He wants to be first in our lives, and He expects us to be moving faithfully in that direction. But He doesn't demand that we become full-blown mature Christian in an instant. We mentioned Romans 8:1 earlier this week. What does it say?

_____

If God doesn't condemn you, then don't condemn yourself. When you mess up, repent and ask God for forgiveness. Then accept His forgiveness and be thankful that He loves you no matter what. God is full of grace. He's not a critical parent demanding perfection.

The more you rest in His love, the more you'll want to please Him in the way you live your life. Saturate yourself with His Word, and He will use the truth to set you free from sin. Just remember, He sees you with eyes filled with mercy and love. Try to see yourself through His eyes.

Procrastination

I wonder how many pounds I've gained because of procrastination? I'd hate to even think. This has been one of my last holdouts in the eating-when-I'm-not-hungry category. The boundaries have helped, yet I still struggle with procrastination.

Fortunately, God can do anything. If He can help *me*—an unscheduled, anti-writing, let's-have-fun sort of person—write a book, then He can help *you* do whatever you need to do!

I don't know how many times I sat down at my computer to write this Bible study, thinking, *I can't do this. It's too hard. If God really wanted me to write this Bible study, He'd make me enjoy writing.* I literally had to journal the truth over and over again to get myself to work on this book because the lies were so deeply ingrained in me.

If you struggle with procrastination, you probably believe some lies as well. Let's look together at some of the things we tell ourselves that keep us stuck in this energy-draining cycle. Circle any of the lies you struggle with, and write the truth below each lie. If you need help, see page 163.

Lies that make us procrastinate

1. It's too hard.

2. I can't do it.

3. I don't have time to do it.

4. I will never be able to please _____ so I might as well not even try.

5. I can't do it perfectly, so I might as well not even try.

6. It's better not to try at all than to try and fail.

7. I don't want to do it (and that's a good reason not to do it).

8. I'll do it later.

9. I'll feel more like doing it later, so I'll wait until I feel like doing it.

10. I work best under pressure.

It really helps when you're dreading a task to check out your thoughts. What are you saying to yourself that's making you so reluctant to begin? After you replace the lie with the truth, you should feel better. Sometimes it will be enough to actually make you look forward to the task. If not, there are some other tricks you can use.

One is to break down a big project into small manageable chunks and then focus on only one step at a time. For example, if the project is losing weight, just focus on following your boundaries for a week, praying Scripture every day, and journaling any time you eat outside of your boundaries. At the end of the week, set another goal.

If the project is painting the bedroom, just focus on getting all the things together that you need for painting. Don't even think about painting until you've completed that task. Breaking big jobs into small jobs will help you to view the project in a different way. It won't seem so overwhelming, so you'll be less inclined to procrastinate.

Another thing you can do is to set a timer for 15 minutes. No matter how terrible the job is, you can handle it for 15 minutes. I use one of those little portable timers that you buy in the kitchen gadgets department. When the timer rings, I often reward myself with something.

In the old days, my reward might have been a bite of cake or ten chocolate chips. Now I reward myself with ten puzzle pieces or a few pages in a book. This reward is better for my figure and less addictive. (And no, I didn't always stop at one bite or ten chocolate chips!)

The timer and reward help to jumpstart me. I don't use them all the time, but I do use them to start a really dreaded task. I used to make myself do one hour of work before I had my second cup of coffee in the morning and that helped too.

Another thing that helped me was to change the expectation that I had to have a large block of free time at my disposal in order to do a project. With four kids at home, I didn't even have a *small* block of uninterrupted time available. It was a revelation to me that you could do a big messy project in bits and pieces rather than all at once.

My friends taught me this lesson. They would get out the paintbrush and paint their living room or kitchen for half an hour. That idea would never have crossed my mind. To me, painting was an all day job. Since that seemed way too intimidating—not to mention boring—I never painted anything. They all complained about my monotonous white walls.

Well, I adopted their tactics eventually and realized that you can paint a room in little blocks of time. It's actually easier to do this in many regards because it doesn't seem like such an overwhelming project. Emotionally, I can handle painting one wall more easily than I can handle painting the whole room. Then when I get started, I often think, *Well, this isn't so bad*, and end up painting the whole room anyway.

Now if you're one of those organized, on-the-ball people, you'll think this whole discussion of rewards and timers and painting one wall is pathetic, but if you're a procrastinator like me, I can tell you that this works! In fact, I have written the last page of this study while sitting in the car at my kids' play practice, waiting to pick them up. That is much better than sitting at the bakery eating a cinnamon roll thinking, *I could never write a whole book.*

God can change you in this area. Do the truth journaling for things you're avoiding, and then try some of the practical ideas. Overcoming procrastination will bring great peace into your life, not to mention all the cookies it will keep you from eating!

DAY 5

Have you ever asked yourself, "How did my life get so busy?" Today we'll look at five questions you can use to evaluate your life. There may be some simple things you can do to make your life less stressful. As you go through these questions, apply them to the areas of your life that overwhelm you.

1. Is this something I can do better?

By better, I don't mean more perfectly. That will only add more stress to your life. However, you may be able to do something more efficiently. The better the systems you have in place to run the routine areas of your life, the less stressful your life will be. Here are a few questions you can ask to improve the out-of-control areas of your life.

First, is this an area you tend to procrastinate? If so, look over yesterday's lesson again and try some of those ideas.

Second, do you need to become more efficient? For example, grocery shopping used to take up a lot of my time until I determined to only go once a week. I keep a standard list in my purse that I use to make sure I don't forget anything. It's hard to force myself to go out once a week for a big shopping trip, but well worth the effort.

Finally, would it help if you delegated more? You might think it's easier to do the cooking and cleaning yourself rather than train the kids to help, but in the long run, you'll be helping yourself *and* your kids if you require them to do chores. It's not good for kids to be waited on. Helping with the chores will teach them that the world doesn't revolve around them, that work is a part of life, and that they have a responsibility to contribute to it. If you're a perfectionist, you may need to lower your standards a bit, but that will be good for you.

Can you think of any areas of your life that you could do "better" in order to reduce the stress in your life? What could you do differently?

_____

_____

2. Is this something I need to do "worse"?

Yes, I know that sounds crazy, but I'm talking about perfectionism here. Is it really worth the stress to do everything perfectly all the time? Lowering your standards can raise your standard of living.

Can you think of any areas of your life that might be enhanced by relaxing your standards? If so, what could you do differently?

_____

_____

3. Do I need to adjust the amount of time I spend on this activity?

All week we've been talking about the importance of keeping God first in our lives. This is difficult to do while living lives so busy we can hardly think straight. Just as emotional eating has become normal in our culture, so has the busy, harried life.

• Why do you think a busy life is held in such high regard in our culture?

_____

• How do you think God feels about the pace that we live our lives? Give biblical support, if possible.

_____

_____

Do you ever feel like you're too busy to spend time with God and others? If so, what could you do to change that?

_____

_____

It's easy to fill our lives with activities. We each have different temptations in this area depending on our interests. The person who thrives on accomplishment may spend too much time working and neglect relationships. The person who loves to have fun may spend too much time on recreation and fun relationships, while neglecting service and ministry. And the person who just wants peace may not be willing to step out of her comfort zone to get involved in the things God wants her to be involved in.

We don't stop to evaluate the way we live our lives because the world says it's okay for us to focus on our passions. In fact, it's not only okay, it's desirable. We can't be happy if we're not getting our needs met, right?

They forget to tell us that the best way to get our needs met is to develop a close walk with God. Only He can truly fill us up. We don't need to make time to pursue our passions. We need to make time to pursue Him.

Often it's the pursuing of our passions at the expense of doing what God wants us to do that makes our lives so stressful. Let's take a moment then to examine our lives.

List all the activities you do on a regular basis (for example, reading, work, emails, Facebook, texting, exercise, hobbies, wandering around the house, etc.).

_____

_____

_____

_____

Now look back over your list. Are there any activities God might want you to spend less time on?

_____

If so, why do you think He wants you to spend less time on them?

_____

_____

Sometimes we're busy because of circumstances we can't change. Perhaps you're a single mother, or maybe you have a special needs child that requires a lot of your time and attention. You may have elderly parents to care for, or you may deal with health problems of your own that are difficult. Many are in financial situations where you have to work, even though it makes life stressful.

If God has allowed you to be in this position then He'll give you the strength to see it through. It may be hard to make time with Him a priority, but that's what you need to do. Ask Him for the strength and wisdom to handle your situation in a way that honors Him, and rest on His promise that He can bring good out of all things.

If your life is busy and there's nothing you can do about it, can you think of any ways to bring God into your regular life? (For example, meditating on Scripture throughout the day, praying on the way to work, doing one truth journal at lunch, visiting with Him throughout the day, etc.)

_____

_____

_____

4. Is this the right time of my life for this activity?

• We've been taught by our culture that it's possible to "have it all." Do you think that's true? Why or why not?

_____

• If it's not possible to have it all, then we have to decide what we're going to have and what we're not going to have. How do you think God would want you to decide what activities get to stay and what activities have to go?

_____

_____

If life is about loving God and loving our neighbors, then the activities we allow into our lives should focus on those two things. Who are your most important "neighbors" at this stage of your life? Are you spending enough time with them?

_____

Those of us who have kids at home must be very careful to guard our time. It's our duty to love our kids, pray for them, and do all we can to help them develop godly character and a lasting relationship with Jesus Christ.

In order to have time for this, we may have to say no to things we'd really like to do. This may include recreational activities, hobbies, jobs, and even ministry opportunities.

This hit home to me personally when I first started working on this Bible study. There were a few weeks there that were very stressful for my family because I was trying to do too much. I had to learn to set realistic goals for my writing and say no to other activities, so I could keep my family as my priority and still have time to write and teach this study.

How about you? Do you have any "neighbors" that you need to be spending more time with? How can you adjust your schedule so that you have more time for those relationships?

_____

_____

5. Am I trying to please the right One with this activity?

Do you ever find yourself with a too-full schedule just because you have a hard time saying no? It's easy to get swept up into a life of people pleasing because we want others to like us, and we think they'll be mad at us if we say no.

If you struggle with people pleasing, consider using the people pleasing or living up to expectations questions in *I Deserve a Donut* to renew your mind before saying yes to activities that will require a big time commitment. I also have some questions on my blog called "Decision Making and God's Will: 14 Questions to Help."

It's so easy to go through life just saying yes to everyone without stopping to ask, "What does God want me to do?" Or "What are my most important priorities at this time in my life?" Or "Who do I want to make sure I have enough time for?" Knowing what's important will help us say no to the things that aren't important.

Think of your own life. What (or who) are your most important priorities at this stage of your life?

_____

Do you feel like you're spending enough time on (or with) those priorities? If not, what's getting in the way?

_____

_____

Can you think of anything you're doing only because someone expects you to do it?

_____

If so, do you think this is something God wants you to do? Why or why not?

_____

_____

The flip side of living life to please others is living life to please ourselves. When we feel like we absolutely have to have "me" time or that we absolutely have to have time to work on our goals, we'll feel stressed when the normal demands of life get in the way. It will bother us when other people put demands on our time because they're getting in the way of our goals.

The solution to stress really comes back to the principle we learned at the beginning of the week: The more we put God first in our lives, the less stressed we'll be. When we seek to please Him rather than ourselves or others, we can live in peace no matter what the circumstances.

• We've looked at many ways to reduce stress in our lives. If you could change one thing about your life to make it less stressful, what would it be?

_____

If the change is something God would approve of, why don't you try to do it?

Depression, Loneliness, and Celebration

Clara entered the elevator and pushed the button. Another long day visiting her husband, and now, home to an empty apartment. As the elevator ascended, her mind drifted back to the days when their kids were little. If only she could turn back the clock, she thought. Life used to be so good. The elevator arrived at her floor, and Clara got out. The hall was quiet. She opened the door to her apartment and set her purse on couch. As she took off her coat, she pictured her husband getting ready for bed at the nursing home. She wondered if he'd ever be able to come home again. Probably not, she thought . . . but it was easier not to think. Clara fixed herself a snack and turned on the television.

Do you ever feel like life is just too hard? It's easy to get depressed when life gets the best of us. This week we'll talk about depression and loneliness and then end our study on a positive note with celebration.

The causes of depression are many. It might be a catastrophic event. It might be a physical problem. Or it might be a negative emotion that you've held onto for too long. If I wallow in my discontentment, for example, or hold onto my anger for months on end, I'll probably end up depressed.

We also get depressed when we dwell too much on the past, have difficulties in the present, or dread the future. That's what we'll discuss in this chapter.

If you're struggling with chronic depression, please see your doctor or a counselor. There may be a physical reason for your depression, plus it's just helpful to have another person come alongside you and give you help from time to time.

DAY 1: The Past

There are two temptations we have when looking at the past. Either we idolize it and long to have it back, or we think about what we *should* have done, regretting past actions that are causing our current pain. We'll address both of these problems today, using the questions we learned in the worry chapter: *Do I need to change the way I think? Do I need to act? Do I need to submit?*

Do I need to change the way I think?

God is good all the time. We've heard these words before, but have you ever really thought about them? How would believing those words make a difference in your attitude if you were longing for the past?

_____

_____

• Do you remember our options charts in chapter two? Longing for the past is dwelling on an option that doesn't exist. Why do you think longing for the past would lead to depression?

_____

When we're longing for the past, it's hard to be grateful for the present. All our thoughts are focused on how much better life was "back then," and it's difficult to clear our minds.

What advice does Paul give us in 1 Thessalonians 5:16-19?

_____

• If you were to develop a habit of always being thankful—in other words, making a conscious effort as you go through your day to thank God for specific blessings—how do you think that would affect your overall attitude towards life? If you already have a habit of being thankful, how does that attitude affect your life?

_____

_____

Why don't we try giving thanks right now? Take ten minutes and begin thanking God for everything you can think of. Be specific. Instead of saying, "I wish I could have the old days back," say, "Lord thank you for that trip we took to the ocean. It was such a blessing to run on the beach."

Instead of saying, "I was so stupid to make that decision," say, "Lord, thank you that you work all things out for good. Thank you for what you've already taught me through this trial and what you'll continue to teach me. Thank you that you're enough. That I don't need the perfect life. Thank you for your goodness."

Thank Him for the blessings of the past. Thank Him for the blessings of the present. And thank Him for His blessings in the future. After you're through, describe your experience.

• How do you feel after thanking God for 10 minutes?

_____

Another way the past can make us depressed is when we think about what we *should* have done. We can't live perfectly, and we can't make perfect decisions. There will be times in each of our lives where we'll think, *I wish I had done that differently.* Is that an option, though? Can we go back and do things differently? Of course not! It's useless to dwell on what we should have done.

How does dwelling on what you should have done negatively impact your life?

_____

You can't go back and change the past, but you do have choices in the present. Try making an option chart to see if that will help. It's also comforting to know that God can redeem any situation. What does Romans 8:28 have to say about this?

_____

Past actions are easy to regret if they're causing current problems. It helps to remember that God can use these problems in our lives to help us grow.

Think of a problem you're experiencing because of past actions. Can you think of any ways God can use this experience to build your character? Are you allowing Him to do that?

_____

_____

Can you think of any ways God has equipped you to minister to others because of your experience or any other good things He has brought into your life through it?

_____

_____

If your past actions hurt another person or caused them to stumble, can God still work in that other person's life and bring good from the experience? (Read Romans 8:28 again if you need to.)

_____

Do I need to act?

Although we can't go back and change the past, we do have options in the present. Think of your own regret. Do you need to apologize to anyone? Is there anything you can do to make amends? Would it help to write a letter? If you need to ask forgiveness, avoid making excuses for your behavior. Give a humble apology.

Can you think of any actions you need to take?

_____

If you're longing for the past, you may need to take some actions to change the present. Rather than focusing on what you *should* have done, ask yourself, "What can I do now to make my current life (or future) better?"

How would you answer that question?

_____

Life may be different now, but it can still be good. Draw near to God, give Him thanks, and pray about a new direction for your life.

Do I need to submit?

This is an important question to ask ourselves if we're dealing with regret over the past. If we never get to the point where we accept that this is just the way life is, we'll never break free from our depression.

We may need to say, "God, I don't like this, but I'm willing to live any sort of life for You," and then embrace that life. Or we may need to say, "Lord, I wish my actions had been different, but I can't change them now. I release this situation to You, knowing that You can bring good out of any situation."

As I write this chapter, I'm going through my own major life change. Our oldest son went to college this past year, and I'm still adjusting to it seven months later. In fact, that's what turned me in the direction of writing this Bible study because I now have more time on my hands.

I've loved these years with my kids and am grieving the day that they'll all be gone. Yet I know that God will help me adapt. He'll give my husband and me another sort of life that will also be good. I'll have more time to minister to others and plenty of time to love God and commune with Him. Life will be different, but different doesn't have to be bad. If I keep God first in my life, and not my husband or kids, it will be easier for me to adapt.

The bottom line is that I need to submit. This is what God has for me. Kids grow up and leave home. I need to release my son to the Lord and do the same for the other kids when they're ready to go. And I need to release that old life to the Lord and be ready to take what He has for me next.

How about you? Is there anything in your life that you've been clinging to? Is there anything you need to accept about your current life?

DAY 2: The Present

Let's face it. Sometimes life is devastating. We lose someone we love. A serious illness is diagnosed. A sudden event catapults us into the unknown. When things like that happen, the grief can be so intense that it's hard to imagine ever being happy again.

Yet God is there in the midst of the pain. He's reaching out to us, waiting for us to come to Him so He can wrap His arms of love around us and soothe away the hurt. It will be easier to rest in His love if we take the time to look at the situation from His perspective.

Do I need to change the way I think?

If you want to read a perfect description of depression, read Lamentations 3:1-33. This book was written after King Nebuchadnezzar conquered Judah and destroyed the temple. The author of this lament was devastated. He poured out his feelings to the Lord, and we soon see a lifting of his spirit.

At what point in this passage does the message change from one of despair and depression to one of hope, and what is the reason for his hope?

_____

I love verses 22 and 23. Write them on the lines below.

_____

_____

Why are we not consumed by our difficulties? Because of the Lord's great love for us. Because of His compassion. Because of His faithfulness. He is with us in the hard times. He is with us when no one seems to care. He is with us when we're depressed. We have hope because *He is with us.* When we start putting our hope in other things, we open ourselves up to more depression.

Think for a moment. What are you putting your hope in? A Relationship? Success? A lifestyle? Financial security? Becoming a perfect person? If we put our hope in earthly things we'll get depressed when those things fail us.

What circumstances tend to make you depressed? In what ways are you putting your hope in those things rather than in God?

_____

_____

How would it change your life and your attitude about life if you were to put your hope in God? Or if you're already putting your hope in God, how is that affecting your outlook on life?

_____

_____

God is waiting to soothe our pain. The more we go to Him for comfort, perspective, and help, the more content we'll be.

Read Lamentations 3:25. Who is the Lord good to?

_____

If we hope in God and seek *Him,* we'll find that He is good. If we hope in earthly things and seek easy ways of escape, we'll probably feel like He is not good. Remember that life doesn't have to be good in order for Him to be good. He can use hard things to help us grow when we get our minds off our pain and onto His provision.

Read Lamentations 3:31-33 and James 1:2-4. Trials often lead to depression, but depression itself is also a trial. Can you think of any good things that could come out of the trial of depression? If you're depressed right now, what could God teach you through your current trial and the trial of depression?

_____

_____

If life seems bleak to you right now, that doesn't mean it will always be bleak. What does Psalm 30:5 say?

_____

_____

• Can you think of another time in your life when you were depressed, but God brought something good out of your pain? Was the suffering necessary? What blessings did He bring into your life through your trial?

_____

_____

Sometimes we're depressed, but we're not really sure why. Here are a few questions you can ask yourself to look for reasons behind your depression.

1. Is there an out-of-control emotion in your life? For example, are you constantly worried, are you having a hard time forgiving someone, or are you struggling with insecurity, envy, pride, or judgment?
2. Could you be under spiritual attack?
3. Is there anything in your life that you're making more important than God wants it to be?
4. Are you involved in a sin, expecting God to make you happy, even though you're unwilling to give up your sin?
5. Are your expectations for life too high? Have you bought into the culture's idea that life has to be wonderful in order for you to be happy?
6. Are you dwelling in the past, wishing you had made different choices or wishing you could have the old days back?
7. Are you in a situation that you can't change, that you just need to accept?
8. Are you dwelling on the good, remembering to be thankful?

The answers to these questions may point to the reasons behind your depression. Because this is such a complex emotion, it can be hard to figure out. Please seek professional help in overcoming this emotion if you need it!

Do I need to act?

Sometimes we just need to act. Make some sort of life change that will help us feel better. Here's the question we can ask ourselves: Is there anything I can do that God would approve of to change my situation? The key phrase here is "that God would approve of."

If I'm depressed because of my marriage, God's not going to approve of an affair. If I'm depressed because of my finances, God's not going to approve of a trip to Hawaii. If I'm depressed because of my weight, God's not going to approve of a pig-out session.

Still, there may be things we can do to make life more enjoyable. Think of the situation that's weighing you down. Can you think of any changes you could make to improve it? Also, would it help to talk your problems over with a counselor?

_____

_____

Depression can also be improved by exercise and healthy eating habits. Do you think this could be an issue for you? If so, what could you do to help?

_____

Do I need to submit?

Is there some unchangeable situation in your life that you just need to accept and give up to God? Or are you in a situation that is changeable, but you know God doesn't want you to change it? Sometimes life is hard to accept, but it's what we need to do to gain peace and move on.

If you're struggling with depression, believe that God will bring good things from your trial. Maybe not as soon as you'd like, but it will happen! Renew your mind. Give thanks. And above all, hope. He will use this for your good.

Think of your own life. Is there anything you need to accept? If so, how would your life and attitude change if you were to let it go and just accept it?

_____

_____

DAY 3: The Future

If you're depressed about the future, you probably have reason to believe the future won't be bright. Worrying about the future makes it harder to enjoy the present. Fortunately, God has provided answers in His Word to help us handle our worries.

Do I need to change the way I think?

Read Paul's advice to Timothy below and then make a list of dos and don'ts based on the passage.

Instruct those who are rich in this present world not to be conceited or to fix their hope on the uncertainty of riches, but on God, who richly supplies us with all things to enjoy. Instruct them to do good, to be rich in good works, to be generous and ready to share, storing up for themselves the treasure of a good foundation for the future, so that they may take hold of that which is life indeed.

1 Timothy 6:17-19 (NASB)

Do:

1._____

2._____

3. _____

4. _____

5. _____

Don't:

1. _____

2. _____

Why are we to "do the dos" and "not do the don'ts"? (1 Timothy 6:19)

_____

We have to constantly remind ourselves that life is not about security, comfort, riches, entertainment, or anything else we might try to make it about. Life is about God! Our hope, then, is not in a certain lifestyle, but in God.

What does Jesus say in the following verses?

Matthew 6:33-34 _____

_____

Matthew 22:36-39_____

_____

If life is about loving God and others, will it be so terrible if we lose our health, our jobs, our dreams, or even our freedom? Can we still love Him in those situations? Can we still love others in those situations? The answer is yes. No matter what happens, we can still love God and others. And if that's what life is about, then we have no reason to be depressed about the future.

• How do you think having this mindset would affect your thoughts about the future?

_____

_____

Do I need to act?

Is there anything you can do right now to make the future brighter? Don't let worry and depression paralyze you. Take one small step toward a better future.

If you're worried about your health, what can you do today to improve your health for the future?

_____

Is there anything else you should be doing to make your future better? If so, what?

_____

_____

Do I need to submit?

If God allows something to happen and we can't do anything about it, then we need to accept it. Only then will we begin to grow and learn what God wants us to learn from the situation. It's fruitless to worry about what we should have done or fret about the future. God is in control. In our distress, we can cling to His promises: He uses all things for our good (Romans 8:28), and He is our refuge, our strength, and an ever-present help in trouble (Psalm 46:1).

DAY 4: Loneliness

In the age of social media, many people are lonelier than ever. Listen to this quote by Mother Teresa in her book, *A Simple Path: "The greatest disease in the West today is not TB or leprosy; it is being unwanted, unloved, and uncared for. We can cure physical diseases with medicine, but the only cure for loneliness, despair, and hopelessness is love. There are many in the world who are dying for a piece of bread but there are many more dying for a little love."*

Loneliness is painful. To feel that no one cares for you is to feel completely alone, even if you're in a room full of people. Yet Someone does care. You are never alone.

Do I need to change the way I think?

God loves us. We can see an example of the kind of love He loves us with in Hosea 11:1-9. Read this passage and record on the lines below, the things God did and the things Israel did in return.

God did: _____

_____

_____

_____

Israel did: _____

_____

_____

The book of Hosea is difficult to read. God loved the Israelites. He longed to be in relationship with them, yet they kept ignoring Him and running after idols. It's hard to read because it reminds us of all the times in the past when we've done the same thing.

There's no reason to ever be lonely, because God is always there. We may not feel close to Him for a number of reasons. Perhaps we're holding onto a sin that's causing distance. Or we're running to other things for comfort rather than Him. Or maybe we're just not spending enough time with Him to feel close. If we want to have a deep relationship with Him, we need to earnestly seek Him. Relationships like that don't come easily.

Do I need to act?

If you're feeling lonely because you're not close to God, the best thing you can do is work on your relationship with Him. He always wants to be in relationship with you, and He never dies or moves away.

Often we feel lonely because of the loss of a close relationship. Our loved one may have died, he may have moved, or he may just not want anything to do with us anymore. That's hard. Often our only choice in those situations is to accept it with a good attitude or a bad attitude. But sometimes there is something else we can do. Maybe we need to apologize or put more effort into the relationship, or maybe we need to change in some way so that we're easier to be around.

If you're in one of those situations right now, is there anything you can do to make it better? If so, do you think God wants you to do that? Why or why not?

_____

Loneliness is a perfect opportunity to reach out to others. What does Peter tell us to do in 1 Peter 4:9-10?

_____

Only God can fill that empty spot that's inside of us, but ministering to others will also help. Is there someplace you could volunteer? How about helping teach kids how to read in the schools? Or visiting people in the nursing homes or the jails?

Does the church have a ministry for you? Is there someone in your neighborhood you could reach out to? Any mothers with young children who need help? Any homeschoolers you could offer a class to?

Look for hurting people. Look for lonely people. Look for busy people who need help. In the process, you'll become less lonely yourself.

Jot down some ideas on the lines below of people you might be able to reach out to or ministries you could get involved in.

_____

_____

Do I need to submit?

Friends move. Kids leave. Loved ones die. Those are the sad but true facts of life. We need to be willing to give these dear ones up to the Lord and be grateful to Him for our current blessings—even when they don't feel like blessings. There is freedom in submission.

Is there anything in your life you haven't accepted yet? If so, how is it contributing to your loneliness and discontent?

_____

_____

In many ways, prayers of thanksgiving (Philippians 4:4-6) are prayers of submission because we're choosing to praise God and focus on His goodness in the midst of our pain. If you're having a difficult time accepting a situation that seems unacceptable, try praying a prayer of thanksgiving. When I do this, I always find that God changes my attitude.

DAY 5: Celebrations

How many times have you been doing well with your boundaries, only to be sidetracked by a celebration of some sort? Parties, holidays, vacations—they're hard on boundaries. It's almost like having an excuse to eat.

• What are we thinking that makes us believe it's a good idea to eat huge quantities on these occasions?

Overeating during holidays, vacations, and celebrations is such a part of our culture that it's hard to imagine anything different. Let's look at some lies we believe about eating on these occasions.

1) I can't have any fun if I have to watch what I eat.

Is this true? While it may be fun to eat during celebrations and vacations, it's not fun to step on the scale the next morning.

Can you think of any other unpleasant consequences of eating too much during celebrations and vacations?

One of the worst things about eating too much on holidays and vacations is the potential it has to derail us. So often we're going along great, sticking to our boundaries, and then here comes the holiday and—boom—all of a sudden we're struggling again. We can save ourselves all that trauma by continuing to follow our boundaries all the time.

If we were to ask Jesus what our focus should be during parties, vacations and holidays, what do you think He would say?

Ouch! Sometimes it's painful to stop and look at what we do through His eyes, isn't it? I think He would say that people are more important than food and that glorifying Him is more important than stuffing our faces. Parties should be about relationships, not about indulgence. (I'm feeling convicted as I write this!)

2) It's not fair if others get to eat all they want, and I don't.

As we go through life, we have to make all kinds of decisions: *What will I do for a living? Where will I settle down? Should I get married? How should I spend my time today? What should I have for dinner?* We base our decisions on different things.

For example, if I'm trying to decide what shirt to buy, I'll base my decision on how much it costs and how I look in it. It would be ridiculous to base my decision on how good my friend looks in it and whether or not it fits into *her* budget.

It would be just as foolish for me to decide how much to eat based on how much my friend is eating. What if my friend eats a whole rhubarb pie and a carton of ice cream? Should I eat just as much as she does? What if she eats half the pie and half the ice cream? Then should I eat as much as she eats? Of course not. What's good for my friend isn't necessarily good for me. Not to mention the fact that all that pie and ice cream isn't really good for her either.

• What would be some good things to base my eating decisions on?

_____

• What would be some bad things to base my eating decisions on?

_____

As you can see, what I eat should have nothing to do with what others eat. That's a truth I'll need to drill into my head if I want to eat responsibly when others are around.

3) I shouldn't have to suffer when everyone else is eating.

There's no doubt you'll suffer if your friend is eating a treat right in front of you and you're not eating. But here's the interesting thing. You'll also suffer if you break your boundaries and *eat* the treat.

How will you suffer if you break your boundaries?

_____

How will you suffer if you follow your boundaries and say no to the treat?

_____

Which decision will cause more suffering? Explain.

_____

Is short-term pleasure worth long-term regrets? _____

The truth is, we don't have to suffer when others are eating in front of us. It's a free world. We can eat if we want. The question is, do we really *want* to eat? Either way, we suffer. Or to put a positive slant on things, either way, we're rewarded. Here's a question we can ask ourselves when we're in those tempting situations: *Would I rather be rewarded with five minutes of fun, or would I rather be rewarded with a lifetime of health, freedom from the control of food, and all the other benefits I receive from a life of consistently following our boundaries?* When you ask it that way, I think I'll take the boundaries.

4) It would cramp my style to follow my boundaries on a vacation.

This implies that following our boundaries is a bad thing, but is it? Don't boundaries protect us? What if every time I went on a vacation I flirted with all the men I came in contact with? Would that be good for my marriage and my life? Of course not!

There's no reason to break good boundaries that protect us and enhance our lives just because we're on vacation.

Boundaries by their very definition mean that we can't do everything we want. In fact we have them in place so we don't do everything we want! And let's face it, doing everything we want isn't always the wisest course we could take, is it?

• Can you think of any good reason why you shouldn't have boundaries in the area of food when you have them in other areas of your life?

My friend, we need boundaries, and we need to follow them—*especially* when it's unpleasant to do so.

5) It's too hard to follow boundaries on holidays.

It's hard to follow boundaries on holidays. There's no doubt about it. Christmas is especially difficult since it lasts so long and tends to be stressful. If you eat for stress or procrastination, Christmas would be a dangerous time for you even without extra treats around.

Your best bet is to rely on God as much as possible throughout the holidays. Try praying through the Bible verses on page 53 twice a day and truth journaling whenever you get stressed out. This will help. You may also want to look at practical things you can do, such as limiting the number of treats you have in the house or getting your holiday to-dos done early so you're not tempted to eat for procrastination.

• Can you think of any other practical ways to reduce temptation during holidays?

Celebrating Progress

There's something sad about ending a book. Even though we're not really doing it together, in some ways it seems like we are. I may have written the study, but I'm still going through it with you as I continue to work on these things in my own life. It's nice to have the camaraderie of working together, isn't it?

If you've made it this far, you have reason to celebrate. You are further along on your goal of breaking free from the control of food than you were at the beginning of the study. It may not seem like it, especially if you're still struggling with following your boundaries, but you are. Truth makes a difference. And you have more truth under your belt now than you did eight weeks ago.

As you finish this study, I want to encourage you to keep pressing on, even when you'd like nothing better than to give up. God will set you free from emotional eating, but it takes time.

Continue going to Him for help with life. Renew your mind. Abide in His Word. And give thanks in everything (even failure). He who began a good work in you will complete it! And when He does, it's sure to be wonderful.

Appendix A

1. I'll start being faithful to my boundaries tomorrow.

If past experience is any indication, there is about a 5% chance that I'll follow my boundaries tomorrow if I break them today. My best chance of being faithful tomorrow is to be faithful today.

2. Eating is fun.

Eating a reasonable amount is fun. Eating too much is not fun. It makes me feel uncomfortable, lethargic, and unhappy. It also makes me gain weight, which isn't fun.

3. I can't stick to my boundaries. I have no self-control.

If emotional eating is a stronghold for me, then self-control won't work. Only the truth can set me free. If I want to follow my boundaries, I'll need to keep going to God for help and apply the truth diligently to this area of my life.

4. Just one little bite won't hurt.

Although *one* bite won't hurt, past experience has taught me that I won't stop at one bite. There's a 1 in 100 chance that I will truly eat only one bite. It's more likely that I'll end up eating the whole thing, which will lead to eating more things. And this one little bite will end up hurting quite a bit.

5. I don't know when I'll get _____ again. I better eat it now.

There is almost always a way to get _____ again if I really want it. I would be much happier if I ate it only when it fit into my boundaries.

6. I've been following my boundaries perfectly for *two weeks* and haven't lost anything. These boundaries don't work.

If I've really been following my boundaries perfectly, I may just need to be patient. It could be water weight. If the problem persists, it would be helpful to speak with a health care professional to see if I need to adjust my boundaries.

It's also possible that I haven't been following my boundaries well enough to lose weight. If I stick to my boundaries all day and just cheat a little bit each night, it will take longer to lose weight. I'll still *feel* like I'm following my boundaries because I'm following them for most of the day. Unfortunately, I need to be good for the whole day in order to lose weight.

7. I already broke my boundaries. I might as well eat _____.

The sooner I stop the better. One bowl of ice cream is better for me than one bowl of ice cream and four cookies. If I stop now, I probably won't have eaten enough to gain much weight, if any. If I keep going, though, I could pack in a lot of food in a short time. It would be a *victory* to stop at only one bowl of ice cream.

8. I've been so good at following my boundaries that I deserve a treat.

If I have a treat, then I won't deserve it anymore because I *won't* have been good at following my boundaries. Also, if my goal is to lose weight, then breaking my boundaries is a punishment, not a reward.

9. Eating will make me feel better.

Eating will only make me feel better for a short time; then it will make me feel worse.

10. Maybe I'll sleep better if I have something to eat.

It might make me sleep better tonight, but overall, eating too much will make me sleep worse. I'll sleep better and have more energy if I maintain a healthy weight. Spending time with God will help me sleep better, too, and it will be good for our relationship.

11. It's only dough; it's hardly even a cookie.

Dough has just as many calories as cookies. For all practical purposes, it really is a cookie.

12. I want it (and that's a good reason to have it).

If I did everything in life I wanted to do, I would be in big trouble. "Wanting to eat" is not a good reason to eat.

13. I'm on vacation (at a party, etc.). It's okay to eat.

It's okay to eat if I want to gain weight! Even on vacations, it's good to have boundaries. I can modify them and eat a little more than usual, but I should still have some sort of boundary so I don't go crazy and eat everything in sight.

14. I'll feel more like doing _____ if I have something to eat first.

The longer I wait to do something, the harder it is to do. In reality, eating will make me feel apathetic and lazy, and I'll want to do it even less.

15. It will go to waste if I don't eat it.

If it's not good for me, I'm still wasting it by eating it. In fact, you could say I'm wasting it even more because it's actually doing harm rather than just being wasted.

16. I don't eat that much. I just have a low metabolism.

In order to know if this is true, I would need to measure and record everything that I eat and drink for at least a couple of weeks, even if it's just a lick of the spoon. Then I would need to add up the calories and compare them to what I should be eating to maintain my weight.

It's possible that I don't know what appropriate serving sizes are. I may also be forgetting to count the calories in what I drink, and I may even be eating without realizing it.

If I find that I'm eating the right amount to lose weight and still can't lose it, then I should speak to a professional for help. I may need to start an exercise program to increase my metabolism.

17. I'm so tired. Maybe a treat will perk me up a little bit.

A treat would only perk me up for thirty minutes or so, if that. Afterwards I will be just as tired, if not more so. In the long run, I will be less tired if I exercise and eat well on a regular basis.

18. This is so good that I should have another piece.

This is so good that I should thoroughly enjoy the first piece. The second piece never tastes as good as the first. It is far better to *really enjoy* one piece (with half the calories) than to really enjoy one piece, kind of enjoy the second piece, and feel bad about eating so much afterwards. This is also a good reason not to have that second serving!

19. I gained _____ pounds this weekend.

Chances are, a good portion of the weight gained is water weight that will go away in a couple of days of normal eating. It takes 3500 extra calories to gain one pound. In other words, if I need 2000 calories a day to maintain my body weight, I would need to eat 5500 calories in one day to gain a pound that day.

So if the scale says that I gained three pounds over the weekend, I really didn't unless I ate an extra 10,500 calories. In like manner, if the scale says I lost three pounds, some of that may also be water weight. In order to have lost three pounds, I would have had to have a shortfall of 10,500 calories between exercise and eating less.

20. I will never be able to lose weight and keep it off.

I will never be able to lose weight and keep it off in my own strength. But I can do it through Him who strengthens me.

It's not determination and self-control that will keep the weight off, but a mind held captive to God. I must bring my thoughts to Him for renewal on a regular basis. As He changes the way I think, I'll lose my desire to overeat and eating with boundaries will become a way of life.

This is what will help me to lose weight and keep it off. All things are possible with God!

Appendix B

Week 2: Day 3

	Happiness	God	Changing Bill
1. Divorce Bill.	?	↓	---
2. Nag at Bill - try to get him to change.	↓	↓	↓
3. Do the work but punish Bill in other ways.	↓	↓	↓
4. Do work with "poor me" attitude.	↓	↓	↓
5. Do work and eat ice cream.	↑↓	↓	↓
6. Do work cheerfully, submitting to the Lord and forgiving Bill.	↑	↑	?
7. Forgive Bill and have kids help with the work.	↑	↑	?

Week 5: Day 4

Beliefs: 1. Life is so boring 2. All I ever do is change diapers and break up fights. 3. If only I had a job, then I would be happy.

Truth: 1. True, although there are moments of excitement every once in awhile. 2. Actually, that only makes up less than 5% of the day. There are many wonderful moments with my kids also. 3. If I had a job, I would have two rat races—one at work and one at home. Plus my home time would be much more rushed as I tried to get everything done in a short amount of time. Being home with the kids is a privilege. Sure, there are some moments that aren't easy, but that is true of everyone's life. I shouldn't expect it to all be easy. These kids are precious, and God has entrusted them to me. May I be the mother that God wants me to be.

World	God
Life should be fun.	Life is fun at times—but it doesn't *have* to be fun. That's not what life is about. It's about loving God and loving others. In living this out, sometimes I will have to do things that aren't fun.
I deserve to be happy.	I am a sinner and I deserve death, but God has given me the free gift of eternal life (Romans 3:23 and 6:23). I am to seek Him and His kingdom *first*, not my own desires (Matthew 6:33).
I shouldn't have to work this hard—life should be easy.	Jesus warned us that our life would be hard (John 16:33). I should expect to have to work hard sometimes. The easy way is not always the best way or the right way.
I need to find my soul mate in order to be happy.	I need to submit to the Lord in all things and spend enough time with Him to develop a close relationship with Him—only then can I be truly happy.
If only I had a (bigger house, nicer car, skinnier body, different husband, better job, etc.), then I would be happy.	- See above - Plus 1 John 2:15: *Do not love the world or anything in the world. If anyone loves the world, the love of the Father is not in Him.*
I can't be happy if I'm not living my passion.	I can't be happy if I'm not living for God. He should be my passion. As I become passionate about Him, He will give me things to do for Him that will also be satisfying to me.

Week 7: Day 4

Lies that fuel perfectionism:

1. This has to be perfect to be acceptable.

I can only do my best, and it will never be perfect. Only God is perfect, and He doesn't demand perfection from me. He loves me just as I am.

2. I'm a failure because I (failed in some way).

I'm a sinner saved by grace. I *will* fail from time to time because I'm not perfect. Thankfully, I'm not defined by what I do, but by who I am in Christ. And He doesn't see me as a failure. He sees me as a beloved child of God.

3. I can't start this project until (the rest of my life is in order, I know exactly how to do it, I have a large block of time available for it, etc.).

Chances are, my life will never be in order, I'll never know exactly how to do it, and I'll never have the time to do it the way I want to do it. If I'm going to do it, I must begin now under imperfect conditions.

4. If it can't be done well, it's not worth doing.

I can't learn to do something well until I've done it poorly a few times first. Also, God might want me to do some things to the "pretty good" level so that I have more time to do other things well.

5. If I'm perfect, people will love me, admire me, accept me, etc. If I mess up, they'll be mad at me.

I will never be perfect! They'll have to love me as I am if they're ever going to love me. My job is to love them and ask forgiveness when I sin against them. I can't control what they think of me. And even if they hate me, God will still love me.

6. It's terrible if I make a mistake.

It's *life* if I make mistakes. Everyone else makes them—why should I be exempt?

7. People expect that of me. I need to live up to their expectations.

God wants me to please Him, not others. I am *not required* to live up to the expectations of others. It is *okay* if they're mad at me.

8. If I want something done right, I need to do it myself.

If I want something done *my way*, I need to do it myself. But things don't have to be done my way, and I shouldn't expect others to do things my way. Of course they will make different decisions, and that is all right. God wants me to be flexible.

9. I'm a bad Christian if (I don't go on a short-term missions trip, I'm not a bubbly person, I don't lead a Bible study, I'm not perfect, etc.).

I am not defined by what I do, but by who I am in Christ. And in Christ, I am a child of my Father, the King of the Universe. A beloved daughter created for the works He wants me to do—not for the works everyone else thinks I should do. As I die to self and live for God, He will be molding me to His image. I am a work-in-progress.

10. I should have known better.

I can't make perfect decisions all the time. Sometimes I'll do the wrong thing, and sometimes I'll make the wrong choice. It's inevitable. But God is sovereign and full of grace. He'll work all things together for good (Romans 8:28).

Lies that make us procrastinate

1. It is too hard.

It is hard, but not too hard. I can do hard things. Since it is so hard, I better break it down into more manageable chunks and get started on it right away. I know from experience that the longer I wait to do it, the harder it seems to get in my mind.)

2. I can't do it.

I can't do it easily, I can't do it perfectly, but I can do it. Also, I can do all things through Him who strengthens me (Philippians 4:13).

3. I don't have time to do it.

This truth will depend on your situation. If you truly don't have time for it, and it isn't important to do it now, then take it off your to-do list. If it's important, the truth is, "I must make time for it." Breaking a big job into smaller jobs may help you fit it into your life more easily.

4. I will never be able to please _____ so I might as well not even try.

It is not my job to please _____. It is my job to please the Lord. If He wants me to do this job, then I need to do it even if I know someone will be critical of how well I do it. If appropriate, I could ask my critical person for input so there is a better chance of the job being approved.

5. I can't do it perfectly, so I might as well not even try.

If this were the way everyone felt, then no one would do anything—because we are all imperfect people! There would be no books to read, no houses to live in, and no movies to go to. The truth is, that of course I can't do it perfectly, so I might as well accept that I can't do it perfectly and just do the best that I can.

6. It's better not to try at all than to try and fail.

Failure is the pathway to success. I can't expect to be good at everything right away. If I learn from my mistakes and don't give up, failure can help me succeed.

7. I don't want to do it (and that's a good reason not to do it).

If God wants me to do it, I should do it whether I want to or not. Also, sometimes I need to do what I don't want to do so I can do what I do want to do.

8. I'll do it later.

90% of the time, when I say I'll do something later, I don't do it. If I want to do it, I better do it right now. The longer I wait, the more I will dread it.

9. I will feel more like doing it later, so I'll wait until I feel like doing it.

In reality, I will probably never feel like doing it.

10. I work best under pressure.

I actually force myself to do it under pressure. This doesn't necessarily mean I do it better. Sometimes, I'm forced to do a poor job because I don't have enough time to do a good job. Often I am frazzled and grumpy with those around me when I operate this way because I am under *too* much pressure.

Lie/Truth Chart

The chart on the following page can be copied and used to renew your mind when you eat outside your boundaries. After filling each page, review your entries, then turn it over and write down any general principles you learned on the back of the paper. You'll be surprised by what you learn about yourself, the lies you believe, and the reasons you eat.

You may also want to journal any time you weigh yourself and are disappointed with the weight or any time you're feeling hopeless about your weight.

I'll show you a couple of examples from my own lie/truth charts, and then you can use the empty chart on the next page for your own chart. Be sure to make copies, as you will go through a lot of pages before you get rid of all the lies you believe about eating!

Situation	Belief	Truth
Bored, working all day.	1. I always feel like a treat in the afternoon so I should just plan for one. 2. One little treat won't hurt.	1. I feel like eating for emotional reasons. I should plan a *quiet time* in the afternoon. I don't want to be an emotional eater. 2. 95% of the time, it does hurt. Breaking my boundaries a little causes me to break them *a lot.*
Stress - Book not going well. Ate snack.	I'll just have some ice cream now and then have soup for supper.	98% of the time, when I break my boundaries once, I end up breaking them a bunch. I've got to get this into my head. I should have said, "I think I'll just forget about my boundaries and eat as much as I want today and regret it tomorrow," since that's what eating a bowl of ice cream in the middle of the afternoon will do to me.
Went to a potluck with fabulous desserts.	1. These desserts are so great. 2. I should have another one. 3. After all, when will I have another opportunity like this?	1. True. 2. I'll have to be careful not to have another one, since it would be easy to break my boundaries and I want to live a life of following my boundaries. 3. I can have an opportunity like this whenever I want it if I ask the person who made them for her recipe.

Situation	Belief	Truth

Other Books by Barb Raveling

I Deserve a Donut (And Other Lies That Make You Eat)

This is a renewing-of-the-mind resource book. It contains 150+ Bible verses and 36 sets of questions you can use in the midst of temptation to help you actually *want* to follow your boundaries. It also provides a great structure for having conversations with God about life and food.

Taste for Truth: A 30-Day Weight Loss Bible Study

This is a 30-day Bible study that will help you jump-start your weight loss program. Whereas *Freedom from Emotional Eating* focuses on the emotions, *Taste for Truth* focuses more on the weight loss process. It is an in-depth look at our attitudes toward boundaries, body image, and food. It is designed to be used alongside *I Deserve a Donut (And Other Lies That Make You Eat)*.

The Renewing of the Mind Project

This is book about going to God for help to change the things in your life that you feel like you'll *never* be able to change. Things like breaking habits, pursuing goals, and breaking free from negative emotions such as worry, anger, and insecurity. The book contains foundational material on the renewing of the mind and also contains worksheets you can use to start your own renewing of the mind project. The final two thirds of the book contains questions and Bible verses you can use to renew your mind and have conversations with God about your habits, goals, and life in general.

If you'd like to hear about future studies, sign up for Barb's author page at Amazon or subscribe to Barb's blog at barbraveling.com.

24751943R00093

Made in the USA
San Bernardino, CA
07 February 2019